# ORCHESTRA!

# ORCHESTRA!

*Foreword by Sir Georg Solti & Dudley Moore*

Jan Younghusband

Chatto & Windus
LONDON

In Association with Channel Four
Television Company Ltd

*This book is dedicated to Malcolm, Jonathan and Declan;
the musicians and production team of 'Orchestra!'; and
the future of Initial Film and Television.*

Text copyright © Jan Younghusband 1991

First published in Great Britain in 1991 by
Chatto & Windus Ltd
20 Vauxhall Bridge Road
London SW1V 2SA

In association with
Channel Four Television Company Ltd
60 Charlotte Street London W1

The pictures of Sir Georg Solti, Dudley Moore and members of
The Schleswig Holstein Festival Orchestra are taken from the
television series, 'Orchestra!'

The television series on which this work is based was
produced for Channel Four by Initial Film and Television
Limited

A CIP record for this book is available from the British
Library

ISBN 0 7011 3739 8

Phototypeset by Rowland Phototypesetting Ltd
Bury St Edmunds, Suffolk
Printed and bound by Butler & Tanner Ltd,
Frome and London
Colour separations by Scantrans, Singapore

# Contents

Foreword – Sir Georg Solti & Dudley Moore    vii

The Orchestra    1

The Baroque 1600–1750    9

The Classical Era 1750–1828    37

The Romantics 1828–1910    81

The Twentieth Century    121

The Piano    165

The Conductor    189

Appendix    209

Acknowledgements    212

Index    213

# Foreword

## Sir Georg Solti & Dudley Moore

Music is a marvel of civilisation. Without it my life would be very much poorer. It has always been my dream to share my love of music with as wide an audience as possible and I was therefore delighted when Initial Television invited me to make a series about the orchestra.

As I have always loved working with young people, I selected The Schleswig Holstein Festival Orchestra, whose members are young musicians from over twenty countries. I was immediately impressed and enchanted by their professionalism, good will and enthusiasm – exactly what we needed for the series. My partner was to be Dudley Moore, whom I had long admired as a wit and brilliant jazz pianist.

So my dream came true. I found myself working with 110 musicians – Hungarians, Americans, Russians, Italians, French, Germans, Japanese, Brazilians – playing the best in music from Bach to Lutoslawski. What better way can there be to create harmony and peace?

Working with Dudley was a delight. We had great fun and became friends. We shared the inspiration which came from this wonderful young orchestra and I have no doubt that you will be equally rewarded as you join us along this great musical journey.

This book is an excellent guide to the journey. I am most grateful to Jan Younghusband, whose work as Music Consultant was a real support to all of us who worked on the series.

*Georg Solti*

This book, so entertainingly written by Jan Younghusband, continues the aspirations of the TV series 'Orchestra!'

Everyone concerned with the programmes had a compelling desire to bring the notion of the orchestra to the eyes and ears of a public as yet unacquainted with the delights of this grand assemblage of musicians, which can give us a sonorous splendour unparalleled by any other musical effort.

I have myself always wanted to share those rewards with all and sundry ever since my parents, my sister, Barbara, and I used to huddle excitedly around our wireless in our back room in Dagenham, tuned in to 'Promenade' and other concerts that came magically from the Bakelite, be-valved box. Perhaps it was this gregarious experience of beautiful things that ingrained in me probably the only way I can experience emotion easily with other people – a harmony of music and souls that I have always longed for and which it has been almost too painful and beautiful to contemplate.

I will never forget the joys of listening for the first time to Bach's Double Violin Concerto or Schumann's Piano Concerto, or the passions of a Brahms symphony. And now it is time to share those joys, to offer them to you – who may never have been led into this particular countryside with quite the same ease that I experienced, so unconsciously, as a youth.

One thing that was of great concern to Sir Georg and me, when preparing for the TV series, was the fact that music must always be the result of excellence – excellence of performance, of interpretation. To that extent, musical activity, and especially that of the orchestra, might appear to be a rarefied and difficult business, which excludes the amateur. But that is not the case. Just as we can watch with joy experts in other fields, we should be able to view and listen to the orchestra with equal gratitude, for overriding a philosophy of exclusivity is the desire to show the orchestra off, to reveal its riches and to let other people in on its not too closely guarded

secrets. We wanted more companions on our trips into these luscious terrains, more people to understand both how and why the orchestra began. What was Man's desire in creating the orchestra, this purveyor of pleasure and gentle tutelage, of beauty, of passion? This little world of friends?

I hope you will enjoy this book by Jan Younghusband. It is a remarkable product of her own delightful enthusiasm.

# The Orchestra

Orchestral music is one of the glories of the world, yet a surprising number of people are not drawn to it. Along with other classical music, they are inclined to think it daunting, too serious and too difficult for them to enjoy. Even if you feel you would like to listen to it and understand it, where do you start?

Initial Film and Television brought together a group of musicians who wished to try to reveal, simply and comprehensively, the power and wonder of orchestral music. The result is a TV series: 'Orchestra!', which looks at the different families of instruments, how they are used in the orchestra and their history, through a selection of works by the great composers – from Bach in the early 1700s to Lutoslawski in present times. It reveals how instrumental music grew from a small group of players huddled round a keyboard instrument into the modern symphony orchestra we know today, made up of over one hundred musicians.

Sir Georg Solti – a Maestro who conducts the world's finest orchestras, and Dudley Moore – a star of acting, wit and the keyboard, were invited to take part in the series as they both combine great humour with a serious classical music background and virtuoso musicianship. Young musicians were drawn from all over the world to form The Schleswig Holstein Festival Orchestra.

The programmes also feature an instrument which doesn't normally appear in the orchestra, except in modern times: the piano, because Dudley Moore and Sir Georg like to play it.

Orchestral music is now an international business. It is quite usual – as the series shows – for an Hungarian conductor, living in England, to go to Germany, to work for ten days with an English pianist, from Los Angeles, and over one hundred musicians of twenty different nationalities, and perform some of the greatest music ever written.

Put any piece of music in front of them – French, German, Italian, Austrian, Polish, Russian, Swedish, Spanish – and they all know what to do, regardless of language or nationality.

But why is this?

Human beings have always wanted to make music – to

*'Nothing is more beautiful than good music.'*
Sir Georg Solti

*'Playing the piano for Sir Georg Solti is a dream come true.'*
Dudley Moore

sing, to dance and play musical instruments. It's a physical thing. Musical sounds can make us feel happy, sad, seductive, philosophical: music touches all human emotions. We are, after all, born with a musical instrument as part of our anatomy – the voice.

Musical instruments have been around ever since man walked out of a cave and blew down an animal bone. Since then literally thousands have been created.

Mastering a musical instrument is highly satisfying. Playing badly can be one of life's most frustrating experiences, bringing out violent feelings of anger and desperation. Many musicians have childhood memories of being locked in a room and forced to practise. But there is hardly a person alive who hasn't played or sung something in their lifetime.

So why should orchestral music be so daunting? Is it that we are frightened to respond to it in a natural way or simply that our first experience of it is alienating and confusing?

Classical composers can appear to be a lot of old men in powdered wigs with obscure names, mostly German, and all dead. The suggestion that their genius is in some way a freak of nature places us in awe of them and makes us feel that their music is either too clever or difficult to understand. We forget that they simply wrote to entertain the audience of their day.

Living classical composers can also be misunderstood because the dreaded words 'experimental', 'atonal' and 'Avant Garde', can label their music as untuneful and inaccessible.

Listening to classical music at a concert is not always a comfortable experience. Having set off with the thrilling prospect of hearing an orchestra playing live for the first time, one can all too easily find oneself trapped in the middle of a row with only a programme to read when bored, and not even a story-line to follow. To fidget, cough, or whisper to a friend

## The Remedy of Music
Music could cure depression, according to the writings of the English churchman Robert Burton (1577–1640) in *The Anatomy of Melancholy:*

Musick is a tonick to the saddened soul, a Roaring Meg against Melancholy, to rear and revive the languishing soul, affecting not only the ears, but the very arteries, the vital and animal spirits; it erects the mind and makes it nimble. Your Princes, Emperors and persons of any quality maintain it in their Courts: no mirth without Musick. (Roaring Meg was a powerful cannon of the time).

inevitably brings a hail of abuse from neighbouring concert-goers, all of whom seem to be classical music experts trained to sit motionless whilst their souls are torn apart by the music.

It is a relatively recent phenomenon that music has been revered in this way. In Mozart's and Haydn's day the audience would most likely have been eating, drinking, chattering or falling asleep – only waking to hear their favourite singer or player.

Listening to music at home is perhaps easier, as you can dance around the living room to the Brandenburg Concertos if you wish. The instinct to do this is not unnatural, as a lot of the music we listen to today, sitting in silent, regimented rows, was originally written for dancing or as background music for a social occasion and played in private houses.

The history of classical music is well documented and labels have been given to each era following precedents set in art and literature, dividing it into manageable periods of time such as Renaissance, Baroque, Classical, Romantic.

It is impossible to say when orchestral music started because it evolved throughout history from many different sources. However, the TV series begins with the Baroque (1600–1750), when composers started writing special forms of music for instruments alone, using the violin family (violin, viola, cello and double bass) placed around a keyboard instrument. The strings formed the heart of the instrumental group – a position they still hold (but without the keyboard instrument) in the modern orchestra.

The word 'orchestra' – the collective name for a group of instruments playing together – comes from the theatre of Ancient Greece, and means 'dancing place'.

Realising that our series could not give the full history of orchestral music, a selection was made of the information we

*'The concert is a polite form of self-imposed torture.'*

Henry Miller,
*Tropic of Cancer*, 1934

*'There are two golden rules for an orchestra: start together and finish together. The public doesn't give a damn what goes on in between.'*

Sir Thomas Beecham

*Left* Hogarth's *The Chorus*

*Right* Clara and Robert Schumann

found fascinating and relevant about the composers, their lives, their music and the instruments played, joining this with the personal views of Dud, Sir Georg, and the band. The intention of this book is to share our experience of this music with you, and give a taste of the rich treasures orchestral music has to offer.

## House Rules and Maxims for Young Musicians  Robert Schumann, 1848

A general selection:

1 Don't be afraid of words like 'theory', 'thorough-bass' and 'counterpoint'. They meet you halfway if you do likewise.
2 There's much to be learned from singers, male and female. But don't believe everything they tell you.
3 Sing regularly in choirs, especially the middle voices. This will make you more musical.
4 Never miss an opportunity of hearing a good opera.
5 Honour the old and welcome the new. Hold no prejudice against unknown names.
6 Don't judge the work on first hearing; that which pleases the most at first is not always the best. Masters call for study. Many things will only become clear to you with age.
7 Have an open eye for life and for the other arts and sciences.
8 If everybody insisted on playing first violin, there would be no orchestras. Respect every musician in his own field.
9 You must reach a point where you can hear the music from the printed page.
10 As you grow older, converse more frequently with scores than with virtuosi.

## Periods of Classical Music
Dates are approximate as all periods of music overlap:

| | |
|---|---|
| The period up to and including Medieval times | up to c.1500 |
| The Renaissance | c.1500–1600 |
| The Baroque | c.1600–1750 |
| The Classical | c.1750–1828 |
| The Romantic | c.1828–1910 |
| Twentieth Century | from 1900 |

# *The Baroque*

## 1600-1750

This chapter looks at the reasons why music for instruments alone began to emerge, concentrating on the development of the string family, the instrumental music of the period and the composers who, in writing it, laid the first foundations of orchestral music as we know it today.

The orchestra as we know it today has developed over the last 400 years. Prior to this, composers mostly wrote music for voices – for church choirs or for court entertainments such as musical arrangements of the latest work by a fashionable poet.

In order to earn a living from their music, composers would need to be employed as a servant by some wealthy patron, be it the Church or a member of the nobility. Although they had to work hard to satisfy the sometimes restricting demands of their employer, the patron had no control over the essential quality of their musical spirit. At least it was a steady job and they were guaranteed regular performances of their music by a resident band of musicians. The size of this band depended on the financial resources of the household.

If the patron liked music, he would provide the best musical resources money could buy. In return, the composer was obliged to supply entertainment by writing anything from dance music for a party to serious religious music for church on Sundays. His other duties included administration of the musicians and teaching music to the patron, the family and members of the court.

It is now impossible to tell how many musicians were employed in courts because they were usually included on a general list of household retainers, and often did other jobs, like gardening. Musicians often played more than one instrument, this being more practical and economical, and a great variety were used at courts all over Europe, at banquets and for dancing. They were also played in theatres to warm up the audience before the main entertainment. In churches, wind and stringed instruments were played to add to the sound of the choir and organ during services. Instrumentalists would adapt vocal pieces which were already familiar

*'Music must be supported by the king and the princes, for the maintenance of the arts is their duty no less than the maintenance of the laws.'*

Martin Luther, 1566

to the audience and show off their skills through clever ornamentation of the melody. It was only a matter of time before instrumental music could hold its own on the concert platform.

It was through opera in the early seventeenth century that musical instruments formed a regular group to accompany voices. Towards the end of the sixteenth century, a small group of intellectual amateurs in Florence – The Florentine Camerata – had set out to revive the ancient Greek style of solo singing. Opera grew out of a combination of these ideas and from the lavish court entertainments, 'Intermedi', which consisted of music, drama, dance and speech. The first opera house opened in Venice in 1637.

In early opera, each song expressed a single 'affection', such as happiness, sadness, grief, or love, and instruments were used increasingly to help illustrate the meaning of the words. If a young maiden was singing of her sadness at the death of her heroic loved one, the melody and instrumental accompaniment would reflect her mood. This was known as 'word painting'.

*Ornamentation*: note or notes added to the main tune for decoration.

*Melody*: a pattern of single notes arranged in musically expressive succession, described more poetically by Mozart as 'the very essence of music. When I think of a fine melody, I think of a fine race horse.'

---

**Word painting:**

the musical illustration of the meaning of words in vocal music, especially the literal meaning of individual words or phrases. Word painting was a prominent feature of Renaissance and Baroque music, although examples exist throughout the history of music. In the simplest cases, natural sounds like birds, thunder, sighing and sobbing are imitated. The shape of the melodic line may illustrate words; dissonance (clashing notes) may be used to indicate pain. In 1625, Joachim

Thuringus classified words that can be 'expressed and painted' into three types:

1 'Words of affection', such as rejoicing, laughing, or the sound of a bird.
2 'Words of motion and place', such as to stand, run, jump, heaven, hell, mountain.
3 'Adverbs of time and number', such as quick, slow, twice, often, rarely.

Up till now, all the voices or instruments in an ensemble had been considered equally important. The 'new' ideal was to have a clear melody with a strong bass accompaniment (basso continuo). The inner harmonies were often improvised on a keyboard instrument, using numbers (figured bass) to indicate which chords should be played, similar to modern guitar music.

The early opera orchestras consisted mostly of strings, and occasionally brass and wind ensembles, with a harpsichord or two lutes and harps to supply the chords. This group of players, often hidden behind the scenes, was used to play incidental music, dance tunes and to accompany the voices. Later, players came out into the open, sitting in a pit in front of the stage, which helped co-ordination, as the musical director could then see what was happening on stage and lead his players accordingly.

One of the earliest surviving operas still performed on a stage today is Monteverdi's *Orfeo* (1607). Claudio Monteverdi (1567–1643) was born in Cremona, where Stradivari and others later perfected the art of violin making. He began his musical career as a viol player and composer of madrigals and it was as such that he was employed, around 1591, by the wealthy Duke of Mantua. He was known as the 'creator of modern music' because he was the first to take on the new styles suggested by the Florentine Camerata. As Musical Director (from 1601) of one of the richest courts in northern Italy, he had unlimited funds at his disposal. In *Orfeo*, Monteverdi was able to use not only a band of strings but also other instruments, including flutes, cornets and trombones – around forty players in all. Not only did they accompany the voice, they also added to the dramatic scene-setting with instrumental dance tunes. It was a sign of how much money was

*Basso continuo:* the use of a rhythmic bass, or basso continuo, was the most characteristic feature of Baroque music. A bass string instrument would take the lowest, most rhythmic line of music, and a keyboard instrument – an organ or harpsichord – would play the same line, but accompany it with chords. To make sure that keyboard players knew which chords to play, numbers representing the chords were written against their line bass (figured bass).

*Harpsichord:* one of several kinds of keyboard instrument used during the Baroque. Shaped rather like a grand piano, only smaller, its sound was produced by plectrums plucking strings stretched horizontally within a wooden case.

*Viol:* an early form of stringed instrument played with a bow, viols came in many sizes. Some were no bigger than a modern violin, others resembled the cello, but since they did not have a supporting spike, had to be gripped between the knees to be played.

available for music in Italy at this time that he could afford so many players. We now look back at this and place great significance on the fact that it resembles the 'orchestra' as we know it today.

Another Italian opera composer, Francesco Cavalli (1602–76), a contemporary of Monteverdi's, took Italian opera to Paris in 1660 but the French didn't like it. Although there were strong links between Italy and France because two French kings married daughters of the Italian Medici family, the French were ready to create their own musical style which resisted Italian influence for over a hundred years.

The most influential patron of music in France at this time was Louis XIV (1643–1715), whose court in Paris became the centre of musical achievement, especially in opera and ballet. The composer who did much to establish the French style was, ironically, an Italian, Giovanni Battista Lulli (1632–87). Born in Florence, he moved to Paris when he was fourteen years old and was first employed as a scullion in a French nobleman's kitchen, changing his name to Jean-Baptiste Lully. A good dancer and mime artist, he also played the violin, harpsichord and guitar and was extremely ambitious, soon finding a kindred spirit in Louis XIV, who eventually made him Royal Composer in 1653. Both gentlemen were fierce disciplinarians, believing that everything, including music, should be well organised and in good taste, reflecting the splendour of the French Court. They both shared a passion for dancing, so it is not surprising

*'I do not write things by accident.'*
Claudio Monteverdi, 1638

*Below* A music party c.1770

that the operas Lully composed had a great deal of purely instrumental ballet music in them. Together the two men formed a force which might be described as a musical dictatorship.

Lully became a very powerful man, a mark of this being that he obtained sole rights to all performances with singing, thus controlling all operatic performances. Dramatic entertainment was all the rage in France. Lully presented sumptuous evenings of opera and ballet, and out of this emerged a distinct French operatic style which differed from that of the Italians because it favoured short, simple songs (not florid arias) and much more dancing. His ballet music was very popular and was later played separately in concerts as instrumental suites – thus, dance rhythms became an important characteristic of French style.

Louis XIV had a Grande Bande, the twenty-four 'Violons du Roi', and a smaller group called, naturally enough, the 'Petits Violons du Roi', of which Lully was the Musical Director. Lully was obsessional about orchestral finesse. He insisted on giving players and singers detailed instructions about how they should perform so that the music could be executed to perfection – with tightness of ensemble and great rhythmic accuracy. No detail was forgotten. In the case of the orchestra he made them all wear the same clothes so they looked like a uniformed group. He also introduced new techniques for bowing stringed instruments, so the players all used the bow in the same direction – a method still used on the concert platform today.

It was Lully who, in a fit of rage, banned the woodwind (crumhorns and shawms, for instance) from playing inside because they made such horrible sounds. The woodwind players knew that without a complete overhaul of their

One of Louis XIV's twenty-four 'Violons du Roi'

Jean-Baptiste Lully

instruments, they would never be allowed back inside. Jean Hotteterre, from a family of French woodwind instrument makers, together with his colleague Michel Philidor, set about redesigning the whole lot – producing new patterns for recorders, transverse flutes, bassoons and oboes. Lully, pleased with the instruments' improved sounds, found room for them all in his opera scores.

To lead the instrumental group Lully beat time loudly on the floor with a large stick. Although this was the French custom at the time, it proved fatal in Lully's case. Known for his outbursts and for screaming at the orchestra, he accidentally smashed his foot with the stick in a moment of passionate frenzy, developed gangrene and died.

English composers, who had previously flourished in Elizabethan England, were hindered in the Baroque period because music was banned in public places during the Civil War (1648–60), making musical development very difficult.

Charles II (1630–85), who had fled to France during the Civil War, had heard the twenty-four 'Violons du Roi' when he stayed at Louis XIV's country palace at Versailles. When the monarchy in England was restored after the war, Charles returned, bringing with him French fashions, music and musicians and a determination to have a similar orchestra of his own. The English, starved of music during the war, were ready to receive these new styles and English instrumental music quickly absorbed the French sound of a central group of string players with added woodwind.

Charles took on players in preparation for his coronation in Westminster Abbey. The twenty-four played at court functions, although they were not allowed at first into the Chapel Royal – that was taking things too far. But Charles had his way in the end. Then in 1663, twelve players were chosen 'to

be a select band to wayte on us whensoever there should be occasion for musick'.

Charles was an habitually late paymaster – it was sometimes as long as seven years before players saw their fees – so when the London theatres re-opened in 1660, the freelance royal violinists lost no time in seeking work there. Usually they performed French-style overtures before the plays started, and a tune between each act, and were generally paid on time.

Oboes were available in London from the mid-1680s (imported from France), the bassoon by 1690 and so for more elaborate theatrical productions, English composers had an orchestra nearly as grand as Lully's at their disposal.

Henry Purcell (1659–95) was a master of beautiful melodies and emotional expression in music, shown particularly in his opera, *Dido and Aeneas* (1689), which he wrote for a girls' boarding school in Chelsea. The work shows influence of French composers in the overture and dance rhythms.

Back in Italy, instrumental music was performed more and

*Chamber music:* the music played in the homes of the aristocracy came to be called 'chamber music' – literally, 'room music'. The term is still used today for music that involves only a small number of players.

*Sonata:* a piece of music written in several movements, usually three, the first and third of which were fast, the second slow. At first the word was used to describe any instrumental, as opposed to vocal, work, but gradually came to imply a work performed on one instrument.

*Concerto:* the word 'concerto' derives from the Latin *concertare*, meaning 'to fight side by side'. During the Baroque there were two main types: the solo concerto and the concerto grosso. The concerto grosso is for a small group of solo players, the 'concertino', playing with a larger group, the 'ripieno' – also called 'solo' and 'tutti' respectively, meaning 'one' and 'all'.

more in its own right, independently of opera. The glorious instruments of the great violin makers of northern Italy – Amati, Stradivari and Guarneri – were used for a variety of compositions, of which the concerto became the most important. There were two main types: the solo concerto and the concerto grosso. The two Italian composers now thought to have developed this form most successfully were Arcangelo Corelli (1653–1713) and, later, Antonio Vivaldi (1675–1741).

Corelli, a violinist as well as a composer, spent most of his life in Rome. He had three very influential patrons – the queen and two cardinals – and came to dominate musical life there at a time when instrumental music was just beginning to become popular, writing nothing but instrumental pieces. His sonatas and concertos were immensely well known, not just in Italy, but also in England and Germany. For the concertos he preferred writing four or five contrasting movements, including dances, unlike Vivaldi, who usually kept to three movements.

Vivaldi was born in Venice and stayed there most of his life, teaching the violin at a special school for poor and orphaned girls, the Conservatory of the Pietà. Vivaldi's girls were excellent players and their concerts were very popular. He was lucky to have this captive group of talented instrumentalists to work with.

Although he trained and was ordained as a priest, he left the church because of bad health, concentrating on teaching, composition and playing the violin (in St Mark's), eventually becoming a highly accomplished virtuoso. Known as 'The Red Priest' because of the colour of his hair, he could be vain and arrogant – perhaps good qualities for a 'show-off' violinist, but traits which made him unpopular with some people.

He is best remembered for his instrumental concertos –

17

around 450 of them. The twentieth-century composer Dalla-piccola remarked, 'Vivaldi didn't write 450 concertos, he wrote one concerto 450 times.' Most are for one or more violins, but at one time or another he experimented with practically everything else available; recorder, flute, oboe, bassoon, even the clarinet (which had been invented as recently as 1690); lute, viola d'amore, cello, mandolin, trumpet, horn.

It was not the number of concertos he wrote which is important, but the form in which he wrote them – generally in three movements, fast-slow-fast. Bach knew Vivaldi's works and transcribed six of his concertos for solo keyboard. Vivaldi also used instruments to illustrate special sounds as in his most famous work, *The Four Seasons*. This is a set of four concertos, for solo violin, strings and continuo, which tells the story of the seasons, imitating birdsong, thunder-storms, skating in winter, barking dogs and rustling leaves.

The concertos were regularly performed at charity concerts in the Church of the Pietà, and, although it was unusual to have an all-female orchestra, there was no doubt they could all play:

> They are reared at public expense and trained solely to excel in music. And so they sing like angels, and play the violin, the flute, the organ, the violoncello, the bassoon . . . Each concert is given by about forty girls. I assure you that there is nothing so charming as to see a young and pretty nun in her white robe, with a bouquet of pomegranate flowers in her hair, leading the orchestra and beating time with all the precision imaginable.

It was Vivaldi's ambition, though, to become a great opera composer and with this in mind he left Venice to work in other parts of Italy and Europe. He wrote about forty-five

*Viola d'amore*: a bowed stringed instrument similar in size to, but slightly larger than, a modern viola. Bach made exquisite use of it in the *St John Passion*.

*Oboe d'amore*: the 'love' oboe, so called because of its warm sound. It was very popular in the Baroque but never became a regular member of the modern symphony orchestra.

operas – not ninety-four as he strenuously maintained – but none met with much success, and he eventually died in poverty in Vienna in 1741.

Throughout the first hundred years of the Baroque period, Germany had taken musical ideas from the rest of northern Europe. The main problem was that, unlike France and, latterly, England, there was no one central and wealthy court with the money to develop music. Neither were there dukedoms as rich as those of Italy, because they had been impoverished by the Thirty Years' War.

In the Church, Martin Luther (1483–1546) insisted that services be taken not in Latin but in the language that ordinary people spoke. He also wrote and used many more hymns and chorales during the service, again sung in everyday language. It was this music that, in the hundred years after the Reformation, inspired other compositions such as organ chorales and preludes.

The new Italian ideas about opera and song reached Germany through the work of Heinrich Schütz (1585–1672). He was sent to Italy as a young man and when he returned to Germany, developed his own highly personal way of making melody and instrumentation express the meaning of the text. But German composers in the seventeenth century did not do much to advance the development of the orchestra. A lot of Schütz's music and that of other composers of the time was for the Church. Even though they used other instruments, the obvious one to use, since so much music was performed in church, was the organ. The Germans excelled at making this instrument, and its place in German composition was more important than anywhere else in Europe.

The most famous keyboard composer in Germany before Bach was Dietrich Buxtehude (1637–1707). There was a

*Organ*: the traditional instrument of the church. The history of the organ dates back 2,000 years, when the Romans used an organ powered by water pressure. Its sound is more commonly produced by wind pumped through its many pipes, which are controlled by one or more keyboards and foot pedals. The pipes are different lengths and named according to their sound – flute, trumpet, etc. The player can combine the different sounds of the pipes by using 'stops' or knobs that can be pulled in or out, in addition to playing the keyboards and foot pedals.

tradition in Germany at this time for public concerts in churches. When Bach lived in Arnstadt he walked most of the 230 miles to hear Buxtehude's virtuoso playing – 'to sit at the feet of the master'.

Despite Germany's comparatively simple musical life, she did develop some musical styles of her own and unexpectedly produced two giants whose work now stands not only as a final landmark of the Baroque period, but as some of the greatest music ever written – George Frideric Handel (1685–1759) and Johann Sebastian Bach (1685–1750). They inherited a church-based, non-orchestral tradition, mixed with French and Italian styles.

Handel travelled to Italy and eventually lived in England, becoming rich and internationally famous. Bach was never as famous as Handel during his lifetime, being best known as an organist and brilliant keyboard extemporiser. His lack of recognition is due partly to the fact that he stayed in one small area of Germany under the patronage of either Church or court. They stand together in history now, however, both being equally famous.

Bach was born into a vast dynasty of musicians – over several generations there were about seventy Bachs registered as musicians of some kind. J. S. Bach was one of the most prolific composers who ever lived, writing over 1500 musical works. He also had twenty children. His music was written mostly in the style of 'counterpoint', the interweaving of independent but equally important musical ideas. Bach also wrote hundreds of

*Counterpoint*: from the Latin *punctus contra punctum*, meaning point against point. A number of various equally important melodic lines combined into a single musical texture.

*Below left* The most famous member of the Bach family, Johann Sebastian

*Below right* Handel's father banned all musical instruments from the house, but the young Handel smuggled a clavichord into the attic and played during the night when he thought everyone would be asleep.

fugues, a form of counterpoint, in which themes imitate each other, entering at the outset one after another, like a round.

Elaborate and highly technical, the fugue featured a lot in Bach's music, especially for the keyboard. His best-known work of this kind is The Well-Tempered Klavier, a set of forty-eight preludes and fugues.

Bach's career divides into three periods according to his place of employment – Weimar, Cöthen and Leipzig. At Cöthen (1717–23) Bach found a music-loving patron in Prince Leopold Anhalt, who was a skilled string player. Since the church of Cöthen was 'Reformed' and there was little interest in church music, Bach, supplied with a regular group of seventeen musicians, turned to writing instrumental pieces. He also wrote little organ music during this time as it's said the organ in the chapel wasn't very good – he wrote many harpsichord pieces instead. In 1718 he went to Berlin to buy a new harpsichord for his patron and there met the Margrave of Brandenburg, who commissioned him to write a set of concertos. The Margrave was a wealthy nobleman who liked to collect the works of living composers and who also possessed his own orchestra of which he was inordinately proud. Even though he was so wealthy, he gave Bach no advance payment for the concertos.

Bach, perhaps suspicious that the Margrave might never pay him, took three years to deliver the music, which was unusual for him. There is no record that the Margrave's orchestra ever played them, although it is generally believed that the Cöthen orchestra did at some point. When the Margrave died the manuscripts were lost, but nevertheless the concertos turned up in a published edition in 1869, one hundred years after Bach's death.

The Brandenburgs are a set of six concertos for various

Born in the same year (1685) within a month of each other (Handel, 23 February; Bach, 21 March), and only thirty miles apart, Bach and Handel never met. They even shared the same eye doctor, who, it seems did more harm than good to both men.

Johann Sebastian was twenty-fourth in the long family line. He himself had twenty children, in order of appearance: Catherina Dorothea, Wilhelm Friedemann, Maria Sophia and Johann Christoph (twins), Carl Philipp Emanuel, Johann Gottfried Bernhard, Leopold August, Christiane Sophie Henriette, Gottfried Heinrich, Christian Gottlieb, Elisabeth Juliane Friederike, Ernst Andreas, Regine Johanna, Christiana Benedicta, Christiana Dorothea, Johann Christoph Friedrich, Johann August Abraham, Johann (there was no shortage of names, but the one before had died at birth) Christian, Johanna Carolina and Regine Susanna.

## The Brandenburg Concertos

| No. | Solo Group (concertino) | Tutti Group (ripieno) |
|---|---|---|
| 1 | violin, 3 oboes, bassoon, 2 horns | strings and continuo |
| 2 | trumpet, recorder, oboe, violin | strings and continuo |
| 3 | 3 violins, 3 violas, 3 cellos and contiuo solo and tutti | |
| 4 | violin, 2 recorders | strings and continuo |
| 5 | violin, flute, harpsichord | strings and continuo |
| 6 | 2 violas, cello | violas, 2 bass viols and continuo |

*'The third Brandenburg concerto is written entirely to be played by strings alone – three violins, three violas, three cellos with basso continuo. Hundreds of years later we play it with a big string orchestra – I did it myself. I performed it with a string orchestra of fifty to sixty players in Chicago. Now we're playing the piece as it was written, with nine solo players and harpsichord continuo, so it is possible to do it both ways.'*

Sir Georg Solti

Bach was always campaigning for extra players and more competent musicians in Leipzig. He wrote a letter to the authorities setting out his ideal requirements:

2 or even 3 violino I
2 or even 3 violino II
2 each – viola I, viola II, violoncello
1 double bass
2 or 3 oboes, according to need
2 flutes
1 or 2 bassoons
3 trumpets
1 kettledrum

Total: 24 musicians in all

Johann Sebastian Bach and his family at morning prayers

combinations of instruments, including strings, trumpet, recorder, flute, oboe and harpsichord, and show how Bach enjoyed experimenting with different instruments.

Other important works to come out of this period were the Concerto for Two Violins (the 'Bach Double') the original manuscript of which was also lost; the four orchestral suites; and the violin concertos.

The post of Kantor of St Thomas's School, Leipzig, became vacant, a prestigious appointment involving responsibilities for musical life in the city, centred in two churches – St Thomas's and St Nicholas's. Luckily, Bach succeeded in getting the job even though he wasn't first choice for it, and stayed in Leipzig for the rest of his life. As a religious man, he was delighted to be back in the church, although he had endless wrangles with the church authorities over pay and conditions. It was during this time that he produced some of his most famous religious music – the *St Matthew Passion* and the *B Minor Mass* – and instrumental works, the Goldberg Variations and The Art of the Fugue.

Because Bach didn't have many musicians available to him in Leipzig, the *St Matthew Passion* and *B Minor Mass* were performed using amateur musicians and boys from the school. Although he may not have had many musicians in Leipzig, we can tell from the complexity of his music that, say, the Cöthen orchestra must have been very competent. Occasionally his music includes a virtuoso part for an unusual instrument, like the horn, which usually indicates that a particularly skilled horn player was in the area.

Handel was probably one of the first truly international composers, absorbing all the styles of the time, German seriousness, Italian grandeur, and French suavity. Much of his music is very witty and entertaining. The word painting

*'I wouldn't have had a profession in Bach's time as an orchestral conductor. The music was conducted from the harpsichord or one of the other instruments, so I would have had to be a player.'*

Sir Georg Solti

*'Bach is like orange juice – every day I come down from bed and play Bach.'*

Dudley Moore

in his operas and, especially in choral works such as *Messiah* and *Israel in Egypt*, is unmatched. For example, in *Israel in Egypt* he uses instruments and voices to describe flies and lice, the drying up of the Red Sea, the slaughter of the enemies, galloping horses, in a highly dramatic way.

Handel saw himself as a great opera composer and went to Italy to study the new styles. His first opera was performed in Florence in 1707 when he was only twenty-two. It was in Italy that he met the man who was to influence the rest of his life – the Elector of Hanover, later to become George I of England. He offered Handel the position of Musical Director of the Hanoverian court, but the audacious twenty-five year old accepted only on condition that he was allowed to visit London first. It was in London that he saw his chance to introduce Italian opera to the English, opening *Rinaldo* in 1711 to immediate success. After this he was reluctant to go back to his job in Hanover and he asked the Elector if he could visit London just once more. He did, in 1712, and stayed for the rest of his life.

When the Elector became England's new King, George I, Handel was frightened he would lose his job because the Elector had been so angry at his absences. The new King held a boating party on the Thames. They sailed down the river on a fleet of barges, had dinner, and sailed back again. A friend of Handel, who wanted him to get back on good terms with the King, persuaded the King to arrange a special barge for fifty musicians, made up of strings, woodwind and brass players, to perform Handel's music. The music apparently delighted the King and was later published as The Water Music. History now tells us that George I had already forgiven Handel and, indeed, had even raised his salary.

GLUCK.

The composer Gluck asked Handel's advice on writing opera. Handel replied, 'You have taken too much trouble over your opera. Here in England, that is a mere waste of time. What the English like is something they can beat time to, something that hits them straight on the drum of the ear.'

*Above* Christoph Willibald Gluck

*Right* George Frideric Handel

*On one occasion when Handel tried to introduce some instrumental variety into his orchestra by using a serpent (a type of wind instrument), he was so disgusted with the sound that he called out in rage, 'What the devil is that?' On being informed that it was a serpent, he retorted, 'Aye, but not the serpent that seduced Eve.'*

Thomas Busby, 1825

*'We talk of a marvellous, brilliant composer and organist, Handel, who lived like a king and died like a king. The funeral allegedly was unbelievable. And there was Bach, living modestly in Leipzig – when he died his music was sadly soon forgotten.'*

Sir Georg Solti

*Oratorio:* a work for solo voice, choir and instruments whose theme is nearly always sacred. The texts are often taken straight from the Bible, or are paraphrases of Biblical stories.

The success of John Gay's *The Beggar's Opera* in 1728 showed that English audiences were tired of grand opera sung in Italian and preferred to hear music sung in English with stories about everyday life. Handel's opera company went bankrupt and he took to composing oratorios – a kind of concert version of an opera, using biblical stories in English – presenting them in London theatres during Lent, when opera performances were forbidden. Oratorios were cheaper to produce than opera because they did not require the same elaborate sets and costumes. These oratorio performances were punctuated with interludes of instrumental music, especially organ concertos and concerti grossi.

Handel had a stroke after the collapse of his opera company and even his oratorio seasons took a while to catch on, not helped by the fact that Queen Caroline died in the autumn of 1737 and all the theatres were closed. But Handel had a good commercial sense and a determination to carry on in the face of all adversity. The English were rather partial to Corelli's string orchestral music, so Handel announced a set of 'Twelve Grand Concertos in the Italian style of Corelli and Albinoni', for sale by subscription, promising to inscribe the front of the score with the name of the individual purchaser. This was a way of securing money in advance of writing the music. Although the response wasn't as good as he had hoped, he decided to continue, writing the whole set in just over a month, in October 1739.

They are written in the typical concerto grosso form – a small group of strings (concertino) and a larger group (ripieno) with harpsichord (basso continuo) – and are all in several contrasting movements, showing the influences of Corelli and the French overture. They were performed during the oratorio season, starting in February 1740, when *Israel in Egypt* was first performed.

Handel had a reputation for being a charitable man, giving his money away to support the poor houses. It may have been for this reason that he was invited by William Cavendish, the Lord Lieutenant of Dublin, in 1741, to take part in a series of oratorios in aid of local charities.

There had been rumours that Handel was unhappy and might leave London. A friend gave him the libretto of *Messiah* to persuade him to stay. He accepted it gladly and wrote the whole work in only twenty-four days, from 22 August to 12

*Concerto grosso*: usually starts with all the instruments playing together. The solo group then breaks free, playing music which is technically more brilliant. The general effect is one of contrasting sounds.

**Twelve Concerti Grossi, op.6**
On 29 October 1739, the *London Daily Post* advertised the concertos 'for sale' by subscription for a sum of two guineas. Handel entitled them 'Grand Concertos' as opposed to 'Concerti Grossi', hoping people would be attracted by the English title and perhaps led to believe that they were 'grander' than anything he had previously written. Only 122 copies were ordered.

Handel would lose his temper if members of the audience arrived late for a performance or talked while it was taking place, sometimes calling out to the culprits by name, which usually made things worse. On such occasions, it is said that the Princess of Wales would comment, 'Hush, Hush, Handel's in a passion.'

*Left* Handel conducting an oratorio from the harpsichord

*Below* Extract from the original score of 'I Know That My Redeemer Liveth' from Handel's *Messiah*

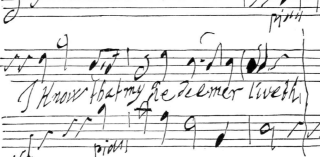

When King George heard *Messiah* for the first time in London, he was so moved that he stood up at the beginning of the Hallelujah Chorus. The whole audience and musicians had to rise also, as the King was standing. Since that time it has been the custom for the audience to stand during this chorus.

September 1741, scoring it at first for string orchestra and two solo trumpets. (Later woodwind were added when it was performed in London.) *Messiah* was first performed in Dublin on 13 April 1742. The tickets cost 'a British sixpence' and the concert raised £400 for charity. The demand for tickets was so great that the ladies were asked to come without hoops in their dresses and the gentlemen without swords, so that they could fit more people into the hall.

As Handel was completing the last glorious years of his life, a new generation of composers was born: Haydn in 1732 and Mozart in 1756. With them, music for the orchestra was to take another important step in its development.

# The Strings

The violin family is made up of four instruments: violin, viola, violoncello and double bass, and between them they form the central part of the modern symphony orchestra.

Their history can be traced back several thousand years, but the modern instruments seen today date from around 1520, with the work of the great violin makers of northern Italy:

Andrea Amati c.1511–80
Giovanni Paolo Maggini c.1580–1632
Nicolo Amati 1596–1684
Antonio Stradivari 1644–1737
Giuseppe Bartolomeo Guarneri del Gesù 1698–1744

Before the beginning of the sixteenth century, players used many different types of bowed instruments, the most common of which were the rebec, lira da braccio and viol. The term 'fiddle' described them all and the bow was called the 'fydyl-styk'.

The violin did not originate from any one of these predecessors, but took on aspects of all of them, with the exception of the viol. This was usually larger and was always, whatever its size, played propped up on or between the player's knees.

After the appearance of what could, for the first time, be called the violin, a whole family of string instruments was developed, which covered the full range and expressiveness of the human voice – soprano (violin), alto (viola), tenor (cello), bass (double bass). It was soon obvious that they were very capable instruments, forming the perfect centre of an instrumental group.

Pythagoras discovered that strings made different sounds according to their length and tension. He found that strings two feet long stretched at the same tension produce the same note. A string half the length produces a note an octave higher. If the string remains the same length and the tension is doubled, it will also sound an octave higher.

It was probably Andrea Amati who set the basic proportions for the violin, viola, and cello, although he began by making three and not four-stringed instruments. His sons, Antonio and Girolamo, continued the business after their father's death, but it was Girolamo's son, Nicolo, who became one of the most prominent violin makers in Italy. He was an inspirational teacher to both Stradivari and Guarneri. It is Stradivari's instruments that are perhaps best known today and, with Guarneri's, are still played by modern virtuosi.

Stradivari copied and perfected the style of the Amati family, making what has come to be known as the 'Long Strad' in 1690. From around 1698 onwards, however, he concentrated on the more common, slightly smaller, 14-inch long violin, which brought him greatest fame. He is said to have made more than 1,000 instruments between the years 1666 and 1737. Of these we know for certain only that 540 violins, 12 violas and 50 cellos are of his own hand. The most famous violins have individual names: Betts (1704); Viotti (1709); Messiah (1716).

Both Stradivari and Guarneri gained their reputation partly from the remarkable musicians who played their instruments. In Stradivari's case it was the violinist, Viotti, and in Guarneri's, Nicolò Paganini (1782–1840).

There is still no explanation for the unique tone of Stradivari's instruments, despite long arguments about his use of varnish and his practice of storing the wood under water. By the late 1700s performance styles had changed so much that the violin needed strengthening. Heavier strings and tighter string tension were needed to produce the stronger, more penetrating sound required to fill the larger concert halls. It was Stradivari's instruments which were best able to take the strain.

The term 'strings' is used for all stringed instruments played with a bow. The strings, together with the harpsichord, piano, harp, mandolin, guitar, etc., are classified under the general heading 'chordaphone', a modern term that encompasses all stringed instruments, with or without bows.

Violin    Viola

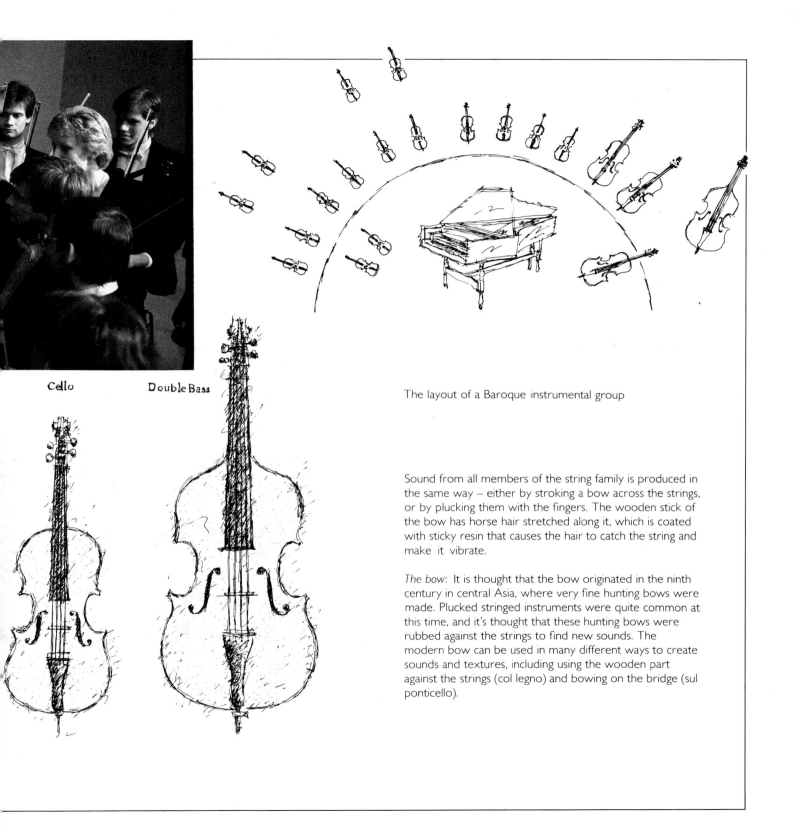

Cello      Double Bass

The layout of a Baroque instrumental group

Sound from all members of the string family is produced in the same way – either by stroking a bow across the strings, or by plucking them with the fingers. The wooden stick of the bow has horse hair stretched along it, which is coated with sticky resin that causes the hair to catch the string and make it vibrate.

*The bow*: It is thought that the bow originated in the ninth century in central Asia, where very fine hunting bows were made. Plucked stringed instruments were quite common at this time, and it's thought that these hunting bows were rubbed against the strings to find new sounds. The modern bow can be used in many different ways to create sounds and textures, including using the wooden part against the strings (col legno) and bowing on the bridge (sul ponticello).

Over the last 300 years, the violin has hardly changed. Any slight alterations in its size and shape have just made it louder and more comfortable to play. The modern violin has four strings, tuned a fifth apart, and the body can be made of various types of wood, including maple, spruce, willow and poplar. With its clear tone and versatility, the violin quickly took its place as the leader of the strings and, indeed, of the whole orchestra. The string players form the central core, and play most of the time. This is only possible, however, because the method of playing the violin makes long passages without a break bearable, whereas a brass player, for instance, simply cannot play continuously for so long.

In the modern orchestra, the violin section, of about thirty-four players, is divided into two, the firsts and the seconds. This does not imply that the second violinists are not such good players as the firsts: composers divide the violins to achieve more variety and a richer texture, although the two sections often play in unison as well. The reason that there are so many violins in a modern orchestra is for the balance of sound – they are needed not only to make a strong sound, but to make an even one, particularly when playing quietly.

The viola, the alto voice of the string family, is shaped like the violin, with four strings tuned a fifth apart, but since it is larger, its tone is deeper.

For many years it was thought that the viola existed before the violin because the name 'viola' was used for a variety of stringed instruments; the viola 'da braccia' ('on the arm') and the viola 'da gamba' ('between the legs'). When a name was needed for the alto of the violin family, 'viola' seemed to fit the bill. But it never lost its connection with 'da braccia', the German word for the instrument being 'Bratsche'.

The viola is known as the Cinderella of the orchestra because

*'In came a fiddler and tuned like fifty stomach aches.'*

Charles Dickens,
*A Christmas Carol*, 1843

According to Sotheby's in London, the highest known price paid for a violin is for a Stradivari, sold for £920,000. The highest price for a viola (sold by Christie's) is £129,000 (Maggini), for a bow (Tourte) £72,000, for a 1698 Stradivari cello (the Cholmondely) at Sotheby's, £682,000, which until recently was the highest price paid for any stringed instrument.

Daguerreotype of Nicolò Paganini, 1840

*'The viola is commonly played by infirm violinists or by decrepit wind players who were at one time acquainted with the violin.'*

Richard Wagner, 1869

it was neglected over the years, eventually finding supporters in Mozart and Berlioz who, in his *Treatise on Orchestration* of 1843, wrote, 'Its low strings have a characteristic husky sound while its high notes are distinguished by their mournful, passionate sound. The general character of its tone is one of profound melancholy.' Berlioz also believed that the instrument's neglect stemmed from the fact that composers did not know what to do with it, writing parts that merely filled in the middle harmonies or copied the cellos and double basses.

Mozart was one of the first to give the instrument an interesting part to play in his Sinfonia Concertante (1779) for violin and viola. It is interesting that he asked for the viola to be tuned higher than usual in order to produce a brighter sound.

Nicolò Paganini, who was famous for the great technical feats he performed on the violin (a Guarneri) acquired a Stradivari viola. A frightening figure, his strange looks and the wild manner of his violin playing made people fear he was akin to the devil. A Stradivari viola was indeed a rare instrument, as he made so few of them. Paganini was keen to display both its rich tone and his mastery of it. As a long-time admirer of Berlioz's music, Paganini asked him to compose something for the viola. Berlioz describes their first meeting:

A man with long hair and piercing eyes and a strange, ravaged countenance, a creature haunted by genius, a Titan among giants whom I had never seen before, stopped me in the passage and, seizing my hand, uttered glowing eulogies that thrilled and moved me to the depths. It was Paganini.

Berlioz composed Harold in Italy (1833) in which the viola characterises Harold – but Paganini was unimpressed, prob-

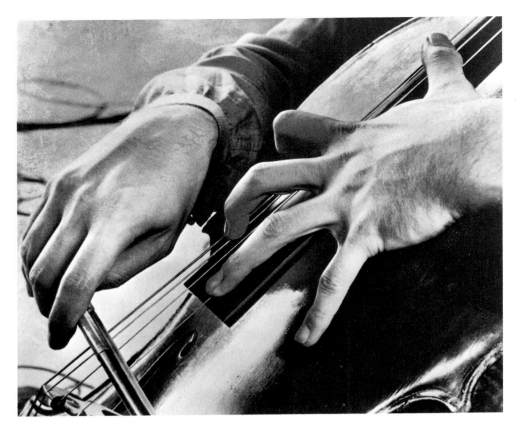

ably because the piece was a symphony and not a concerto in which his virtuosity could have been shown to the full. He paid Berlioz for writing it, even though he never played it.

The third member of the string family, the cello, at first suffered the same fate as the viola, being subservient to the violin, the only difference being that the cello played the bass part in Baroque music, which was of equal importance in the construction of the music to the violin part. Composers once again helped to elevate its status: Vivaldi wrote solo pieces for it in the early 1700s; Haydn, later the same century, wrote two concertos for it, and Beethoven included it in his Triple Concerto, wrote cello sonatas and was one of the first to give it more solos to play in the orchestra. Its highly expressive, rich, singing sounds were especially pleasing to the Romantic composers (1828–1910), who fell in love with the instrument.

*Harold in Italy*: a symphony in four movements lasting approximately forty-two minutes. Berlioz explains why he wrote it: 'In fitting the viola into my poetical memories of my wanderings in the Abruzzi Mountains, I wanted to make the instrument into a sort of melancholy dreamer, in the style of Byron's *Childe Harold*' ('Childe' being a young man of privileged position). Composers have always set to music the words of the admired poets of their time.

Since then, many concertos and sonatas have been written for it, creating a varied solo repertoire that has gained in popularity through performances by famous virtuosi.

The last, and largest, member of the string family – the double bass – also took longer to establish itself as a regular member of the orchestra. This was due mainly to the fact that it co-existed alongside its predecessor, the three-stringed violone. By 1800 the two had merged, keeping the sloping shoulders of the violone, but losing its frets.

In Beethoven's day the double bass was still a three-stringed instrument, and was played by a famous Venetian musician, Domenico Dragonetti (1763–1846) at concerts in London. A mark of his status at the time was that he could command the same fees as the best singers. Beethoven gives the double basses important melodies to play, especially in his Ninth Symphony, where they carry with the cellos, for instance, the main theme of the final movement.

The modern double bass now has four or sometimes five strings. It plays some of the lowest notes in the orchestra and as such, gives a solid rhythmic line to the music. Its light pizzicato (plucked) sounds are ideal for jazz, where it plays improvisatory solo passages ('breaks'). It has been referred to as 'a dangerous rogue elephant', playing the role of the 'Elephant' in Saint-Saëns' Carnival of the Animals, which is one of its most famous solos. Because of its size and character, instrument makers have tried to build larger and larger versions, the largest being by John Goyers in 1889. His 'Grand Bass' stood fifteen feet high and took two people to play it.

*'The cello is like a beautiful woman who has not grown older but younger with time, more slender, more subtle and more graceful.'*

Pablo Casals, 1957

# The Classical Era

## 1750-1828

Now that instrumental music was established in its own right, the orchestra became a unified group of musicians, with woodwind instruments becoming a permanent feature. Special forms of composition were being written for the orchestra alone, most notably symphonies and concertos, and the orchestra acquired a new venue – the concert hall. With the possibility of appealing to a wider audience, some composers took their chances as freelance entrepreneurs, hoping to make a living from their music without the restrictions of patronage from church or court.

The word 'Classical', which is used to cover the period of music history from 1750 to 1828, conjures up something of perfect simplicity of form and of great excellence. The music of this time exemplifies this with a tendency towards formal symmetry rather than emotional expression.

It was a cosmopolitan age – there were French rulers in Italy, German kings in England, and Italian poets working in the German Imperial Court in Vienna, which all served to distribute national styles. J. J. Quantz summed up the new 'international' ideals: 'A music that is accepted and recognised as good, not by one country only, but by many peoples, must be beyond all dispute, the best.' A feeling of universal brotherhood, which was later expressed so vividly by Beethoven in the last movement of his Ninth Symphony, spread throughout Europe. This spirit of liberation was expressed by Rousseau who wrote, 'Man is born free and is everywhere in chains.'

This was the time of 'The Enlightenment' – the name given to a complex movement in the eighteenth century aimed at promoting 'the greatest happiness of the greatest number' through 'the individual revelling in the inner self'.

This new thinking inspired many theoretical publications about science, the history of mankind and music. Between 1751 and 1772, Diderot wrote a twenty-eight-volume encyclopaedia, which he regarded as the sum of human knowledge to date. In 1767 Henri Rousseau wrote a *Dictionary of Music*, and by 1789 Charles Burney had completed the first *History of Music*, in which he said, 'Music is an innocent luxury, unnecessary to our existence, but a great improvement and gratification to the sense of hearing.'

Music publishing became big business, and tutor books were printed from which ordinary people could learn to play

Concerts date back to 6 BC in Babylon, when Nebuchadnezzar's orchestra was made up of horns, trumpets, pipes, lyres, harps and percussion. The Musical Academy in Bologna is another landmark, giving concerts in 1482. In England from 1672, concerts were given in the back room of taverns. Thomas Britten, a coal merchant, converted his loft into a concert hall, charging a shilling a concert. From 1700 onwards, series of public concerts became fashionable, with the 'Concert Spirituel' series in Paris (for which Haydn wrote six symphonies) 1725–84. These were followed by concerts in Boston, New York and London, and many important orchestras were founded as a result.

George III playing the violin at
Buckingham Palace, 1793

the flute, violin, keyboard or sing their favourite songs from
opera. Playing a musical instrument became a social accomplishment, and in 1753 Bach's son, C. P. E. Bach (1714–88),
wrote an *Essay on the True Art of Playing Keyboard Instruments*.

As entertainment became public, composers became
entrepreneurs, presenting public concerts for financial gain.
Sometimes amateur musicians would join in with the professionals on these occasions. Travelling virtuosi went from
city to city organising concerts. Having often been quite badly
paid at court, composers could now make money from their
music, although the freelance life was very precarious, even
for a genius like Mozart. Professional concerts took hold very
swiftly from 1750 and the following 150 years saw the birth of

many of the leading orchestras of today. New concert halls were built and existing buildings were adapted to accommodate the orchestra and its growing audience.

By the mid-eighteenth century there were opera houses all over Italy and Germany and in many other parts of Europe. Italian opera, which was dominated by florid 'da Capo' arias, performed by virtuoso singers paid enormous fees, was no longer fashionable. In these operas, the instrumental music had taken second place to the action on stage.

Christoph Willibald Gluck (1714–87) wanted to restore the dramatic balance in opera by replacing long virtuoso arias with simpler solo singing, linking the musical numbers to suit the drama. He states his views in the preface to his opera *Alceste* (1767). He would 'confine music to its proper function of serving the poetry for the expression and the situations of the plot'. Instruments 'ought to be introduced in proportion to the degree of interest and passion in the words' and 'employed not according to the dexterity of the players, but according to the dramatic propriety of their tone'.

Gluck gave the orchestra a much more important role in his operas, using it for many different effects. The strings play tremolo, pizzicato chords and scale and arpeggio figures and the violas are given an independent part. The oboe, flute and bassoon are given more interesting music, although the clarinets mostly play the same music as the oboe. Horns and trombones strengthen the harmony.

But what happened to purely instrumental music? Chamber music, in the form of the solo sonata (particularly for piano), the string quartet and songs were very popular. Composers created songs out of instrumental music by adding words to existing tunes. These 'parodies' were first produced in the early eighteenth century by C. P. E. Bach and Quantz, and

The 'da Capo' aria was the most important feature of Italian opera at this time, used as a vehicle to show off the virtuosity of the singers. Having sung the aria once through, the singer would repeat it, adding ornaments and using great technical skill. Several of these arias throughout the opera had the effect of bringing the progress of the drama to a complete standstill.

*Tremolo:* the rapid repetition of notes, played as quickly as possible – used for dramatic effect.

*Pizzicato:* a term applied to playing stringed instruments, where the strings are plucked with the fingers.

The longest symphony ever written is thirteen hours long – Victory at Sea by Richard Rogers. A symphony need not always include strings. John Cage wrote a symphony for ten wind instruments (1964). Mozart's father wrote one for four horns, shotgun and strings. Elliott Carter wrote a symphony for three orchestras (1976).

were known by the German name, *Lied* (song). They started out as melodies with a simple accompaniment and, within a hundred years, Schubert had transformed them into highly expressive songs with illustrative piano accompaniment.

The concerto grosso, which had been so popular in the Baroque era, gave way to the symphony and solo concerto, which became the leading forms of music for the orchestra. Many composers contributed to the development of the symphony as the orchestra consolidated into a unified group of instruments.

The term 'symphony' comes from the Ancient Greek word meaning 'sounding together'. It is a kind of sonata for orchestra and grew out of various existing forms: the opera overture, instrumental sinfonias and the concerto grosso. As the Classical era continued the names overture, symphony

## Sonata form

The description of the way music is organised within a movement. This form is often used for the first movement of a Classical symphony:

**Exposition:** the opening part where the composer introduces or 'exposes' the tunes he will use. He invents two themes (or 'subjects') which he may preface with a slow introduction.

*First Subject:* the first tune or theme in the home key (tonic)

*Bridge (transition):* a short passage which develops out of the first subject and changes key joining it to the

*Second Subject:* the second tune or theme (in the dominant key), which usually contrasts with the first.

*Coda:* a short section which ends the exposition.

The exposition is normally repeated. At the end of the repeat comes the

**Development:** the composer takes the two original themes and develops them, taking the listener on an adventure.

**Recapitulation:** grand return of the first and second themes as they were at the beginning, now both in the home key (tonic).

**Coda:** usually longer than the first one, this concludes the movement.

*Right* Extract from Haydn's Symphony No. 99, the 'London'

and concerto were no longer interchangeable and terminology became more precise. It is said that over 16,000 symphonies were written between 1720 and 1810. In the early years of the Classical era, symphony composers often gave the important musical material to the strings, using the wind instruments to reinforce them by filling in the harmonies. As woodwind instruments improved they were often given more important solo music to play in the symphonies.

It was partly due to the work of Johann Stamitz (1717–57) in Mannheim that the orchestra settled into a standard group of musicians. The orchestra maintained by the Elector of Mannheim was generally considered to be the best in Europe. Carl Theodor, ruler of Mannheim, was an extremely wealthy music lover. He employed the young Stamitz as Violin Leader and by 1750 had made him Director of Music. With the encouragement of his patron, Stamitz created an orchestra of individual virtuosi, most of whom were composers in their own right, and between them they set about perfecting the orchestra as a unified musical machine. They were such expert players that the Englishman, Dr Burney, gave them the nickname 'An army of generals, equally fit to plan a battle as to fight it'. Others admired the orchestra's '*forte* like thunder, its *crescendo* like a cataract, its *diminuendo* like the burbling of a brook, and its *piano* like the rustle of spring'. All these things served to make orchestral music more interesting and entertaining.

This orchestra did much to improve the general standard of playing across Europe and it was in Mannheim that the symphony first expanded from three to four movements. Stamitz himself wrote over fifty symphonies and these, together with the compositions of his fellow musicians, were published in London, Paris and Amsterdam.

At Mannheim, the orchestra included pairs of woodwind instruments, and a new instrument, the clarinet. In 1756 the orchestra consisted of 20 violins, 4 violas, 4 cellos, 4 double basses, 2 flutes, 2 oboes, 2 clarinets, 2 bassoons, 4 horns, 1 trumpet and 2 kettledrums. Composers such as Mozart marvelled at the work of this orchestra, especially at the introduction of clarinets as regular members.

Two composers born at the beginning of the Classical era stand out above all others at the time for their extraordinary musical genius as well as for their contribution to orchestral music.

Haydn and Mozart were both born in Austria, Haydn in Vienna in 1732 and Mozart, twenty-four years later, in 1756, in Salzburg. Mozart's short life falls in the centre of Haydn's long and illustrious career.

Franz Joseph Haydn (1732–1809) spent most of his life as a paid servant of the Hungarian court of Esterháza, being released later in life to give public concerts in London, which were hugely successful. He, more than any other, established the symphony as a popular form of entertainment, and the string quartet as a form of chamber music. Haydn is known as the 'Father of the Symphony'. It is now thought that he wrote 106 of them (104 being the previous total) – historians keep finding new manuscripts!

Haydn attributed his originality to his employment at the court of Prince Anton Esterhazy saying, 'I was cut off from the world and forced to become original.' He was relieved to be offered a steady job as previously he had 'to eke out a wretched existence for eight years'.

Prince Anton provided Haydn with a resident orchestra of about twenty-five musicians, and the composer had to report to the Prince everyday at midday to receive his orders:

> My Prince was always satisfied with my works: I not only had the encouragement of constant approval but, as conductor of the orchestra, I could make experiments, observe what produced an effect and make additions or omissions - and be as bold as I pleased.

*Symphony No. 45 or the 'Farewell' Symphony:* Haydn wanted to show his patron that the summer festivities were over and it was time to return to the city. The musicians were keen to see their families again, after a long season in the country. During the last movement of this symphony Haydn instructs the musicians to blow out the candles on their music stands and leave the stage as soon as they have finished playing, gradually decreasing in numbers until there are only two violins left at the end of the piece. Prince Esterhazy understood the message immediately.

Prince Anton died a year after Haydn joined him. His brother, Nicholas, who was also a music lover, took over. After a trip to Versailles, he resolved to build his own palace in the same style and the Castle of Esterháza was built at a cost of about £2 million. It was originally intended as a summer palace, but the prince, accompanied by the entire court, spent more and more time there. The castle had a huge library, art gallery and theatre/opera house, music hall and 126 guest rooms.

Haydn settled into a comfortable, if busy life at the castle. His orchestra gave two-hour concerts twice a week, which resulted in the composer writing twenty symphonies in the first four years of his employment there. The symphonies include many elaborate solo parts for the individual players, giving them a chance to show off their ability to the prince. Haydn took great care over things, and was much respected. For this reason he was nicknamed 'Papa'.

Many musical compositions have been given nicknames over the years, some originating with the composer, but others added afterwards because of some particular characteristic in the music or some event connected with the composition.

Haydn's symphonies are a prime example of this. For instance: the 'Farewell', the 'Schoolmaster', the 'Oxford', the 'Surprise', the 'Clock', and the 'Drum Roll'. All but the last twelve of Haydn's symphonies were written between 1760 and 1788, whilst he was resident at Esterháza, where the orchestra was made up of strings, flute, two oboes, two bassoons, two horns and a harpsichord. Occasionally, trumpets and kettledrums were added. The harpsichord has a particularly important part in the first forty symphonies, and Haydn conducted all his symphonies during the Esterháza period from the harpsichord. Later, in London, he conducted from the piano, which was a new instrument at the time. Of

Joseph Haydn

his 104 symphonies, Numbers 82–7 were written for a special season of concerts in Paris and are known as the 'Paris' Symphonies; Numbers 88–91 were commissioned by private individuals; Number 92, the 'Oxford', was written for Oxford University when he received an Honorary Degree there in 1791. And Numbers 93–104, the 'London' or 'Salomon' Symphonies, were commissioned by the violinist-impresario, Johann Peter Salomon for special concert seasons in London from 1791 to 1795.

The first important symphonies are Numbers 6, 7, and 8, which Haydn called 'Le Matin', 'Le Midi' and 'Le Soir' (morning, noon and evening). 'Le Matin' depicts the sun rising, and the last movement of 'Le Soir' depicts a tempest. In these symphonies he writes special solos for the violin and cello, sometimes devoting a whole movement to one or other instrument. The woodwind are also given more detailed solos, brought into the symphony by Haydn from the outdoor woodwind divertimenti. He also introduces the minuet for the first time, which he later used in all his symphonies, taking great trouble to make sure that each one had its own individual character.

Haydn wrote his symphonies mostly in four movements, starting with a fast movement, followed by a slow movement, a minuet and trio (as one movement) and then a fast finale. In the later ones, he nearly always added a slow introduction to the first movement. He also uses two themes in the first movement, writing in Sonata or 'First Movement' form. Remembering that these symphonies were written to entertain, the order of the movements was designed to take the listener on a journey – presenting the more serious musical material in the first two movements, followed by a relaxing, lightweight minuet and trio, and then a rousing finale. These are the main characteristics of the Classical symphony.

**Divertimenti or Serenades**
These were instrumental pieces composed for private occasions, weddings, birthday parties, and garden parties, using stringed and wind instruments. They particularly suited the woodwind because they sounded better outdoors. Mozart wrote many divertimenti. His most famous serenade is *Eine kleine Nachtmusik* (K.525), which was originally written for string quartet but is now usually played by a small string orchestra.

Between 1771 and 1774 Haydn's symphonies show a darker, more dramatic quality, which was inspired by the German literary movement *Sturm und Drang* (storm and stress), which came about as a result of the philosophies of 'The Enlightenment'. These symphonies are longer than the earlier ones and include effects such as unexpected changes from loud to soft.

Haydn knew very well how to entertain and had a great sense of humour. He knew that his audience would often fall asleep in the slow movements. Symphony Number 94 is now known as the 'Surprise' because it has a sudden loud chord in the middle of the slow movement. Haydn, however, possibly reluctant to offend his public, apparently denied that he had put this in to wake up the London audience.

Haydn's string quartets are as important as his symphonies.

*Above* Haydn playing in a string quartet

*Right* Portrait of Mozart when he was six years old

It was in the quartets that he invented the false reprise – another of his jokes. He would tease his audience by pretending to begin the recapitulation of the main theme (which introduces the last part of the movement) only to change his mind and continue playing around with the other themes a little longer, before the real recapitulation.

Wolfgang Amadeus Mozart (1756–91) had a much harder life than Haydn. He was a child prodigy, travelling all over Europe giving concerts with his father and sister. After a short period of employment by a patron, the Archbishop of Salzburg, he became a freelance composer based in Vienna. He died young and left his family with very little money, only later to be hailed as one of the greatest composers in music history. He excelled in writing all forms of music, especially concertos and sonatas for the piano, string quartets, symphonies and opera. He wrote forty-one symphonies that we know of although, again, some historians now calculate the total as fifty.

Mozart started composing when he was very young. On tour in London in the 1760s, his father became ill and banned all playing of musical instruments in the house because he needed peace and quiet, so Mozart took up composing instead. With the help of J. S. Bach's son, Johann Christian Bach, who by this time was living in London, Mozart wrote his first three symphonies, the first when he was only eight years old, and had written twenty-nine by the time he was eighteen. The first thirty are mostly very short, some only about ten minutes long. He wrote his last three symphonies (39, 40, 41) – which are much longer and more complex – in 1788, within a remarkably short space of time.

Mozart had difficulties finding a job, perhaps because he was too young for senior posts and too accomplished for junior ones. When he was twenty-one his mother took him on a tour looking for work in Munich, Mannheim (where he first experienced the Stamitz orchestra) and Paris, but all to no avail. In Paris he wrote a special symphony 'in the French style' in the hope of appealing to the French audience, but they were still not impressed enough to employ him.

When his mother died, Mozart returned to Salzburg, where his father found him a position at the court in 1779, responsible to the Archbishop. The following year, Munich Court Opera commissioned him to write an opera and the Archbishop released him from his duties in Salzburg to go to Munich to put the opera on the stage. This was *Idomeneo*. The relationship between Mozart and the Archbishop was an uneasy one. While he was working on *Idomeneo*, Mozart was called to Vienna to attend the Archbishop who was visiting there. Although the young composer suddenly found himself mixing in high society, he had to sit at dinner with the other servants, which annoyed him so much that he gave in his resignation. The Archbishop accepted.

Mozart decided to stay in Vienna and try to make a living as a freelance composer, fully exploiting the potential of the new piano to earn a living, composing sonatas and concertos and performing them in public. He wrote music on commission or for special occasions. Between 1784 and 1786, he wrote twelve piano concertos and was in great demand among the aristocracy in Vienna as a performer.

Mozart's concertos are as important for their use of the orchestra as are his symphonies and operas. He established the Classical concerto form, particularly in his twenty-seven piano concertos. In these, the piano is an equal and complementary voice to the other instruments in the orchestra,

particularly the woodwind. These works also show Mozart's outstanding inventiveness.

One of Mozart's great contributions to instrumental music was his genius for writing beautiful melodies that emphasise the singing quality of the instruments. On hearing these melodies it is easy to imagine that he had a singer in his mind when he wrote them. The Clarinet Concerto is one of many examples of this. Mozart is quoted as saying, 'Melody is the very essence of music. When I think of a fine melody I think of a fine race horse.'

It was while enjoying some success in Vienna that Mozart first met Haydn. It was 1781, Haydn was fifty, Mozart twenty-five, and they instantly became friends and admirers of each other's work. Mozart was so inspired by Haydn's op.33 Quartets that he wrote a set of six string quartets himself, which he dedicated to Haydn, and three of which he performed in a private concert in Vienna in 1785. Haydn was present and afterwards wrote to Mozart's father:

> I tell you before God, as an honest man, that your son is the greatest composer known to me either in person or by reputation. He has taste and what is more, the most profound knowledge of composition.

In 1786, the Court Opera in Vienna offered Mozart a commission to write another opera. With the intention of writing a comic opera, Mozart set about looking for a suitable subject and it was during his search that he met the poet Lorenzo da Ponte, who was to become the librettist for many of his future operas. They chose a work by Beaumarchais – *The Marriage of Figaro*. The stage play of this had been banned because it was considered that it poked fun at the aristocracy but, as with

Mozart, his sister, and Leopold their father often toured Europe together, performing in public. Leopold, himself a composer, was very keen that his young son should excel as a musician and subjected him to a heavy schedule of concerts from a very early age.

In 1782 Mozart married Constanze Weber. They had six children but only two survived. Constanze herself was often ill and would regularly visit the spa in Baden for a 'cure'. Because of her absences she is often accused of neglecting her husband, but there is no proof from their letters that they were anything less than devoted to each other.

*Dearest Little Wife!*
*While the Prince is engaged in bargaining*
*for horses, I joyfully seize the occasion to write*
*you a few lines, little wife of my heart! How*
*goes it with you? Do you think of me as often*
*as I do of you? Every moment I look at your*
*portrait and weep, half for joy, half for sorrow!*
*Look after your precious health which means*
*so much to me, my dear, and farewell! Do not*
*be anxious on my account, for I am suffering no*
*hardships or inconveniences on this journey.*
*Adjeu, I kiss you a million times most tenderly,*
*and am ever thine, true til death,*

*stu-stu Mozart*

Mozart wrote a letter to his father on 13 November 1777 complaining that he was paid in watches instead of money:

*What one needs on a journey is money, and*
*let me tell you I now have five watches. I am*
*therefore thinking of having an additional*
*watch pocket on each leg of my trousers so that*
*when I visit some great Lord, I shall wear two*
*watches so it shall not occur to him to present*
*me with another one.*

Leopold Mozart (Mozart's father) to his daughter, 18 April 1786:

*The Marriage of Figaro is to be performed for the first time on the 28th. It will be very significant if it succeeds, for I know there are astonishingly strong cabals against it. Salieri and all his partisans will again endeavour to move heaven and earth.*

*Comic opera:* a new form of opera was created at this time to appeal to more popular taste, moving away from the Italian 'Opera Seria' (serious opera) and into a lighter, comic style – 'Opera Buffa'.

anything that is forbidden, it attracted a lot of publicity. Mozart and da Ponte persuaded Emperor Joseph II that an opera on the subject would cause no offence. Having been granted permission to go ahead, they wrote the whole opera in six weeks. It was a great success. It was after hearing *The Marriage of Figaro* that Haydn resolved not to write any more operas because he knew he could not match the brilliance of Mozart's work. After an invitation to write an opera for Prague in 1787, Haydn wrote a stern note back to the management of the theatre telling them that they should employ Mozart:

Prague ought to employ this man of worth and pay him well; for without such reward, every genius is a sad figure, and this gives little encouragement for others to follow his example. In such a way is great talent lost to the world. It troubles me to think that such an unparalleled being as Mozart is not engaged at an imperial or royal court. Please forgive me for forgetting the purpose of this letter, but I love that man so much.

Although not all successful in his lifetime, Mozart's operas are now considered some of the greatest ever written. After the premiere of *Don Giovanni* in Vienna in 1788, Haydn remarked, 'Mozart is the greatest composer the world possesses.'

Mozart was often a guest at the house of Baron Gottfried von Swieten, a music enthusiast. Every Sunday morning, works by Bach and Handel were played at his house. Mozart wrote to his sister:

'Baron von Swieten, whom I visit every Sunday, gave me all the works of Handel and Bach to take home (after I played them for him). When Constanze [Mozart's wife] heard the fugues, she absolutely fell in love with them. Now she will listen to nothing but fugues . . . Since she has often heard me play fugues out of my head, she asked me if I had ever written any down, and when I said I had not, she scolded me roundly for not recording some of my compositions in this most artistic and beautiful of all musical forms, and gave me no peace until I wrote down a fugue for her.'

As orchestras grew, due to the work of composers in Mannheim, Paris and Vienna, so Mozart's symphonies were written for larger resources. In his early symphonies he uses strings, two oboes, two horns, and occasionally adds two trumpets but by 1782 with Symphony No. 35 the 'Haffner' he was writing for an orchestra of strings, pairs of flutes, oboes, clarinets, bassoons, horns and trumpets, and kettledrums.

An important early work was the Sinfonia Concertante for violin, viola and orchestra (K.364). The form sinfonia concertante, a concerto for several instruments, was particularly favoured in Paris, which Mozart had visited the previous year. When it was first performed, Mozart asked for the viola to be tuned a little higher to make it sound brighter, so it would not be overshadowed by the violin.

While Mozart had been working without a patron in Vienna, Haydn had continued as composer to the Esterháza Court. But his patron, Nicholas Esterhazy, died in September 1790 and the new prince, who was not as interested in music, gave him considerably more freedom. He set off for Vienna. No sooner had he arrived than the impresario, Johann Peter Salomon, offered him work in London. Salomon, a German violinist, had come to Vienna to persuade Haydn and Mozart to take part in his London concert seasons. It was agreed that Haydn would do the first season, and Mozart – who was too busy to do the first – would join them for the second.

When Salomon and Haydn left for London on 15 December

Mozart's works are numbered, prefixed with the letter 'K' (Köchel) after Ludwig Köchel, a nineteenth-century scholar who numbered Mozart's works in order of composition.

Johann Peter Salomon

Mozart had rheumatic fever as a child and was never strong as a result. In the months leading up to his death, he was overworking – on *The Magic Flute* and the *Requiem*, for which he would be paid a lot of money – and his rheumatic symptoms returned. The cause of his death is much debated. Because his body was swollen at death, it was thought he had been poisoned, either by Salieri in a fit of jealousy, or by the Masons for revealing their secrets in *The Magic Flute*. It was common practice at this time to bleed patients to cure illness and it is now thought that Mozart's doctor simply bled him too much. Mozart's burial in a communal grave also causes uproar, but in fact it was the usual form of burial at the time. Joseph II set out rules in his 'Court Decree on Religious and Police Matters' which stated that it was more economical and hygienic to bury several bodies in one grave. It was also forbidden to bury coffins or erect gravestones.

that year, Mozart was in good health but said a strange thing, which a pupil of Haydn's later reported in a letter:

For some time Mozart had a kind of premonition of his death. I remember my master Haydn told me: towards the end of 1790, when he undertook his first trip to London, Mozart said farewell with tears in his eyes, and said 'I fear, my Papa, this is the last time that we shall see each other.' Haydn, who was much older than Mozart, took this to mean that his (Haydn's) age and the dangers which he faced with the journey, gave rise to this fear.

Within a year, Mozart was dead. Haydn at first could not believe it was true. He wrote to Johann Puchberg – a fellow mason who had helped Mozart a great deal in the last years of his life:

For some time I was beside myself about Mozart's death and I could not believe that Providence would so soon claim the life of such an indispensable man. I only regret that before his death he could not convince the English, who walk in darkness in this respect, of his greatness, a subject about which I have been sermonizing to them every single day. You will be kind enough, dear friend, to send me a catalogue of those pieces which are not yet known here and I shall make every possible effort to promote such works for the widow's benefit.

Between 1791 and 1795, Haydn composed twelve symphonies altogether for two concert seasons in London. He shared the leadership of the orchestra with Salomon, who led from the violin, while Haydn 'resided at the piano', often playing the occasional flourish to delight his audience, who loved to hear him play. The orchestra was larger than Haydn was used to, numbering about forty players, almost twice the number he had had in Esterháza. The *Morning Chronicle* reviewed the opening of the first season with great enthusiasm:

> The first concert under the auspices of Haydn was last night and never, perhaps, was there a richer musical treat. Is it not wonderful that to souls capable of being touched by music, Haydn should be an object of homage and even idolatry; for like our own Shakespeare, he moves and governs the passions at his will. His new Grand Overture (a symphony) was pronounced by every scientific ear to be the most wonderful composition. It has four movements – an Allegro – Andante – Minuet – and Rondo. They are all beautiful, and the orchestra performed it with admirable correctness. We are happy to see the concert so well attended the first night; for we cannot suppress our very anxious hope that the first musical genius of the age may be induced by our liberal welcome to take his residence in England.

Haydn returned to Vienna after the first London season and started work on the final six symphonies for the second one. He composed Number 99 in 1799 while his heart was broken over the death of his great friend, Marianne von Genzinger. The slow movement of this symphony, among other works, is thought to be inspired by her. It caused a stir when it was first performed in London because, as the *Morning Chronicle* reported, 'the effect of the wind instruments [which included clarinets for the first time] in the second movement was enchanting; the oboe and flute were finely in tune, but the bassoon was in every respect more perfect and delightful than we ever remember to have heard a wind instrument before.'

Haydn completed his second London season and returned to the Esterháza Court. The new Prince Nicholas wasn't as

Haydn commented on his arrival in London:

*My arrival caused a great sensation throughout the whole city, and I went the round of all the newspapers for three successive days. Everyone wants to know me. I had to dine out six times up to now and if I wanted I could dine out every day; but first I must consider my health and second my work. All this is very flattering to me, but I wish I could fly for a time to Vienna to have more quiet in which to work, for the noise that the common people make as they sell their wares in the street is intolerable.*

(Hadyn lived at 18 Great Pulteney Street, Golden Square, London.)

interested in music as his father had been, the summer palace in Esterháza had fallen into ruin and the family had moved back to Eisenstadt. After his success in London, Haydn found it difficult at first to settle back into his old administrative duties and turned to composing religious works, the most famous of which are *The Creation* and *The Seasons*.

Before leaving London, he had heard a performance of Handel's *Messiah* in Westminster Abbey, performed with a huge orchestra and chorus, which probably inspired him to write these large-scale choral works. *The Creation* was Haydn's first religious work using a German rather than a Latin text. Haydn was shown the libretto for an oratorio based on Milton's *Paradise Lost*, which had been written for Handel, but had never been set to music. *The Creation* was first performed in Vienna in 1798 in the Schwarzenberg Palace, where it was received as rapturously as his concerts in London had been. Copying the style of the successful Handel Festival in London, Haydn used a total of 180 players and it is said that the audience were totally overwhelmed by the scale of the performance. This was the first time that Haydn was truly successful in his home town. Subsequent performances of *The Creation* earned great sums of money for him and he received honours from all over Europe.

In 1808, a year before he died, Haydn attended a special performance of *The Creation* given to mark his seventy-sixth birthday. He was so moved by the warm reception he was given, however, that he had to leave during the interval. As he was doing so, one of his former pupils stepped forward and kissed his hand. It was Beethoven.

Ludwig van Beethoven (1770–1827) was also a child prodigy but was less appealing as a child performer than Mozart because he had a rough-cut personality. He left his home

In the last days of Haydn's life, Napoleon invaded Vienna and the gunfire greatly disturbed Haydn's peace. He would play the Austrian national anthem every day on the piano in defiance of the invaders. By the time he died (May 1809), Vienna was in such chaos that his funeral went almost unnoticed. Later, there was a memorial service and Mozart's *Requiem* was performed.

town, Bonn, in 1786 when he was sixteen and took himself off to Vienna, where he met and played for Mozart. This was five years before Mozart's death. During this time his mother died so he came home and played the viola in the local opera orchestra to help support the family. It was here that he first heard Mozart's operas, *The Marriage of Figaro* and *Don Giovanni*, which he performed regularly with the orchestra.

Haydn visited Bonn on two occasions in the early 1790s on his way to and from London. During this time he met Beethoven and, recognising his talent, took him under his wing. Beethoven managed to get permission to leave his job in Bonn and go to Vienna to study with Haydn – he was twenty-one years old.

The lessons didn't last very long because Haydn left for the second London season. Before he left, though, he wrote to Beethoven's patron in Bonn telling him, 'Beethoven will in time become one of the greatest musical artists in Europe,' and asking for Beethoven's allowance to be increased. It wasn't, so Haydn continued to look after Beethoven, lending him money. He said to Beethoven, 'You give me the impression of a man who has several heads, several hearts and several souls.' After Haydn left for London, Beethoven quickly found other teachers – Salieri and others – and took advantage of the fashion for the new piano by playing, amongst other things, piano variations on a theme of Mozart's opera *The Marriage of Figaro*.

Beethoven is quoted as being quite ungracious about Haydn's support, saying he learnt nothing from him. His formal debut took place in 1795, when he was twenty-five years old, with the performance of his First Piano Concerto. For some time he refused to have his music published so that only he could play his piano works, thus monopolising

When Haydn's body was moved home to Eisenstadt in 1820 they opened the coffin and found his head was missing. Two of his friends had bribed grave diggers to remove the head so it could be kept in Vienna. For over a hundred years the head and body were separated, finally being reunited in 1954.

performances of them. Five years later, in 1800, when he was twenty-nine, he wrote his First Symphony.

In his First Symphony he writes the third movement as a minuet, as was usual in symphonic writing at the time, but gives instructions in the score that it should be played 'Allegro molto e vivace' (very fast and lively). At first this was thought to be a joke but, in his Second Symphony (1803), he replaces the word minuet with scherzo (meaning 'joke') – a movement of racy, wild speed, quite different from the courtly minuet. The scherzo became not only a regular feature of all his symphonies, but also of those of many composers after him.

Beethoven used to take a notebook with him whilst walking in the countryside – one of his favourite pastimes.

> You ask me where I get my ideas from – I can't tell you with certainty; they come unsummoned, directly and indirectly – I could seize them with my hands out in the open air; in the woods; while walking; in the silence of the night; early in the morning; incited by moods which are translated by a poet into words and by me into tones, which sound, roar and storm about me until I have to set them down in notes.

In his late twenties Beethoven came to realise that he was going deaf. Around the time of his thirtieth birthday he became very troubled by this and started admitting it in letters to friends:

(letter to Franc Gerhard Wegeler, Bonn, 29 June 1801)
That jealous demon, my wretched health, has put a nasty spoke in my wheel; and it amounts to this, that for the last three years my hearing has become weaker and weaker. The trouble is supposed to have been caused by the condition of my abdomen.

It is said that Beethoven had three Egyptian inscriptions mounted under glass on his work table. Sir Michael Tippett uses these words in the twentieth century in his opera *A Midsummer Marriage*.

I AM WHICH IS

I AM EVERYTHING THAT IS, THAT WAS AND THAT WILL BE. NO MORTAL MAN HAS LIFTED MY VEIL.

HE IS OF HIMSELF ALONE, AND IT IS TO THIS ALONENESS THAT ALL THINGS OWE THEIR BEING.

Frau von Bernhard, a contemporary of Beethoven, describes the composer:

*When he came to us, he used to stick his head in the door and make sure that there was no one there whom he disliked. He was small and plain looking, with an ugly red, pock-marked face. His hair was quite dark and hung shaggily around his face. His clothes were very commonplace, not differing greatly from the fashion of those days, particularly in our circles. Moreover, he spoke a strong dialect in a rather common manner.*

*'Beethoven is an utterly untamed personality, not entirely in the wrong if he finds the world detestable, but does not thereby make it more enjoyable for himself or for others.'*
Goethe, September 1812

He goes on to describe the various treatments and remedies he tried, none of which did anything to help.

> . . . at a distance I cannot hear high notes or instruments or voices. As for the spoken voice, it is surprising that people have not noticed my deafness; but since I have always been liable to fits of absent-mindedness, they attribute my hardness of hearing to that.

His condition got increasingly worse, and he decided to move to the country, to Heiligenstadt, in the hope that fresh air would finally help him. It was here that he became desperate about the whole problem and entered a period of severe depression. He wrote a very moving letter to his brothers, Carl and Johann, which wasn't found until after his death and is now known as the Heiligenstadt Testament. In it, he describes his anguish about deafness and how he hopes he will experience joy again before he dies.

He lived for another twenty-five years and must have led a tortured life. He was unable to communicate normally with anyone, and finally gave up performing and only occasionally attended social functions because he couldn't hear anyone and this embarrassed him. He would ask people to write in notebooks – which remain now a fascinating account of his life but, of course, only record one side of the conversation.

Always in love, Beethoven had several affairs, but none ended in marriage. Most of his great loves were from aristocratic families and much younger than himself.

With the age of patronage on the wane, Beethoven was, together with Mozart, one of the first 'freelance' composers to write the music he wanted to write rather than fulfilling the requirements of a patron. A group of aristocratic music lovers

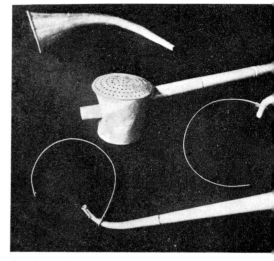

Beethoven's hearing aids, designed for him by J.N. Mälzel, the inventor of the metronome

The exact cause of Beethoven's deafness puzzles doctors to this day. Beethoven himself said it was caused by banging his head one day during rehearsals. A modern view is that he had otosclerosis, which is now an operable complaint, but the post mortem results discount this. Latest medical opinion suggests that he had sarcoidosis, which was caused by being exposed to tuberculosis as a child (his mother died of it). This disease resulted in the general breakdown of his health over the years, with many agonising side effects.

## The Heiligenstadt Testament (extract)

For my brothers Carl and Johann:

*Oh my fellow men, who think or say that I am churlish, obstinate or misanthropic, what injustice you do me! You do not know the secret cause which makes me seem so to you. Ever since I was a child my heart and mind have been filled with tender feelings of goodwill towards humanity: to achieve great things has always been my desire. But you must know that for six years now I have been suffering from a grievous affliction, aggravated by the unskilful treatment of medical men, disappointed from year to year in the hope of relief and compelled at last to face the prospect of chronic infirmity whose cure might take years – if indeed it was possible at all. I was born with an admittance to the ranks of worthy artists and men. You my brothers, Carl and Johann, as soon as I am dead, if Dr Schmidt be still living, request him in my name to describe my malady and attach this written document to his description so that, as far at least as is possible, the world may be reconciled to me after my death. At the same time I declare you two the heirs of my small fortune (if such it can be called); divide it fairly, agree together and help one another. Whatever injury you did me in the past, you know that it is long since forgotten. To you, my brother Carl, I give special thanks for the affection you have shown me of late. It is my wish that your life may be better, more free from care, than mine has been. Recommend virtue to your children, for that alone, not money, will make them happy. I speak from experience, for it was this that sustained me in times of misery, and to it, and to my art, I must give thanks that I did not end my life by suicide. Farewell, and love one another. I thank all my friends, especially Prince Lichnowsky and Professor Schmidt. I should like the instruments from Prince L to be preserved by one of you, but let there be no quarrel between you on their account. If it serves your purpose better, then sell them. How happy I shall be if even in my grave I can be of help to you still. So be it. With joy I hasten to meet death. If it comes before I have had the opportunity to develop all my abilities as an artist then, in spite of my cruel fate, it will come too soon and I shall probably wish it later. Even so, I shall be content, for will it not release me from a state of endless suffering? Come, when thou wilt: I shall meet thee bravely. Farewell, and do not quite forget me when I am dead. I have deserved this of you, for in my lifetime I have often thought how to make you happy. Be so.*

Ludwig van Beethoven, Heiligenstadt
6th October 1802

*(Postscript) . . . Thus I take leave of you, and indeed sadly. Yes, that fond hope, which I brought with me when I came here, that I might in some degree still be cured – that hope I must now abandon entirely. . . .
O Providence, grant me still but one day of pure joy!*

in Vienna supported his work and he sought commissions with great energy.

After the Heiligenstadt visit his spirits improved as he came to terms with his deafness. He wrote to a friend in 1801, 'I will seize Fate by the throat; it shall certainly not bend and crush me completely.' He then entered a period of high activity, usually referred to as his heroic period, and marked by his Third Symphony, the 'Eroica'. When it was first performed, conducted by Beethoven himself in Vienna in 1805, the critics complained that, at over forty minutes in length, it was too long and should be cut. Beethoven had originally designated it 'Grand Symphony' and dedicated it to Napoleon; but, disillusioned and enraged by Napoleon declaring himself Emperor, Beethoven angrily scratched out the dedication, leaving a hole in the title page. It is in four movements, the first an allegro, the second a funeral march, the third a scherzo and the final movement is in variation form – one of his favourite methods of writing.

The distinctive characteristics of Beethoven's style reflect his personal struggle with life. Colin Wilson said of him in *Brandy of the Damned*, 1964: 'He reminds me of a man driving the car with the handbrake on, but stubbornly refusing to stop, even though there is a strong smell of burning.'

Having said this, his music can also be very sensitive and lyrical. We tend to label him as the 'heavy-handed piano smasher' but in fact, in his later years, he developed an inner serenity, born of his years of struggle. This thread of tenderness had always been present in his music. A good example is the slow movement of the Fifth Piano Concerto, written in 1809 and first performed (not by Beethoven) in 1811. His later works reveal a quality of spiritual revelation, including the Benedictus of the *Missa Solemnis*, many move-

Beethoven's friend, Schindler, speaks of visiting Beethoven when he was composing the *Missa Solemnis*. Schindler heard Beethoven stomping round the house, 'singing and howling' the Credo. Beethoven was looking very distressed, obviously not well, and complaining about the state of his domestic affairs. Schindler commented, 'Never, it may be said, did so great a work of art see its creation under such adverse circumstances.'

'You ask me where I get my ideas from – I can't tell you with certainty; they come unsummoned, directly and indirectly . . .'

Ludwig van Beethoven

ments of his last string quartets, and the slow movement of his Ninth, and final, Symphony. When hearing this music one can instantly forgive him for being rude, outspoken and belligerent.

Beethoven is thought of as the herald of Romanticism because his symphonies show every sign of things which were to become important features of Romantic music. He adds trombones to the orchestra, writes descriptive music, increases the size of the orchestra, expresses his personal feelings in his music, uses dramatic changes of dynamics, and the energy in his music gives a feeling of risk, excitement, and unpredictability.

In the Fifth Symphony he writes about Fate knocking at the door – the 'da da da dum' at the beginning being the knocking. It also happens to be the morse code sign for the letter V, used as a symbol for Victory in the Second World War. The Sixth Symphony (the 'Pastoral') depicts country life and includes an orchestral thunderstorm and a cuckoo. The first performance of the Seventh Symphony raised money for Austrian soldiers wounded in the Napoleonic wars. The Eighth Symphony is on a smaller scale than the others, only about twenty-six minutes in length.

Beethoven wrote one opera, *Fidelio*, about a young woman, Leonore, who disguises herself as a man in order to rescue her husband, Florestan, who has been imprisoned for his political views. It conveys the desire to free individuals from oppression and makes a strong statement about courage and freedom. Beethoven had trouble getting it staged as the French army was marching on Vienna. He prepared three versions before it was finally premiered. Because of this, there are three overtures named after the heroine, Leonore, which are often performed as separate concert pieces.

Like Haydn and Mozart, Beethoven also wrote string quartets. The three Rasumovsky Quartets (op. 59) were written for Count Rasumovsky, the Russian Ambassador to Vienna. He was the patron of a string quartet (in which he played the second violin) which was said to be the finest in Europe. To compliment the count, Beethoven uses a Russian melody as the main theme in the last movement of the First Quartet. They sounded so different from previous quartets that people found them at first difficult to understand. A contemporary composer and pianist, Clementi, remarked to Beethoven, 'Surely you do not consider these works to be music?'

The Royal Philharmonic Society was founded in London in 1813 to present concerts, making England an increasingly attractive place for musicians. Beethoven had a very good reputation there – the members of the Philharmonic Society

It's said that when Beethoven saw the marking 'FINE, by the help of God' on the copies of *Fidelio*, he added below the words: 'Man, help yourself.'

were strong supporters of his work. It was eventually agreed that he should write two new symphonies for them. They fought over the fee for five years until Beethoven asked how much they would pay him for one new 'Grand Symphony'. They offered him £50.00 for the Ninth. He accepted and took two years to deliver it.

In the Ninth, he brings solo voices and chorus into the orchestra, to sing the words of Schiller's *Ode to Joy* in the final movement, writing very taxing music for them. During rehearsals for the first performance the singers pleaded with him to change the vocal writing because it was so high. When he refused, one of the singers commented, 'Well then, we must go on torturing ourselves in the name of God.' It was an open secret at the time that the word 'joy' in Schiller's poem really meant 'freedom' – but the authorities had suppressed the use of the word.

Despite the fact that it was written for London, it was first performed in Vienna. Beethoven uses a much larger orchestra than any used by Haydn and Mozart. At the first performance the orchestra consisted of twenty-four violins, ten violas, six cellos, six double basses, the usual woodwind section of flute, oboe, clarinet, bassoon, and included piccolo and double bassoon, four horns, two trumpets and three trombones – a total of around sixty players.

At the first performance on 7 May 1824, Beethoven sat between the violin leader and the conductor, facing the orchestra, with his back to the audience. Moments into the performance he started beating time wildly and it was quite clear that he couldn't hear the music. At the end of the performance he continued his frenzied conducting, obviously not noticing that the performance had ended. The lead violinist rose from his seat and turned Beethoven around so that he could see the

When Stalin heard the last movement of Beethoven's Ninth Symphony performed in Moscow, he said, 'This is the right music for the masses. It can't be performed often enough, and it ought to be heard in the smallest of our villages.' The official art periodical in Moscow wrote: 'Poor Beethoven, for a hundred years he has been homeless. Now at last he has found a true dwelling place – the only country where he is truly understood: the Soviet Union.'

applause. It was quite clear that he was now totally deaf.

A measure of Beethoven's fame and popularity was that 30,000 people attended his funeral in 1827. One of the torchbearers was Franz Schubert (1797–1828). After the funeral, Schubert and some friends went to the tavern where Schubert proposed a toast to Beethoven: 'To him whom we have buried' and then a second glass to himself, 'To him who will go next.' A year later he, too, was dead.

Like Beethoven, Schubert wrote nine symphonies. If Beethoven had died at the same age (thirty-one) he would have only written one symphony. Schubert's music, like Mozart's, was completely mature in his early compositions. He was born in the suburbs of Vienna in 1797 just as Beethoven was writing his First Symphony. Schubert composed *his* First Symphony in 1813, when he was sixteen years old. From a poor family, he couldn't earn a living by performing because he wasn't a virtuoso, so he taught in his father's school and composed in his spare time. Later, like Beethoven, he gave recitals in aristocratic households in Vienna and, aged nineteen, was offered somewhere to live by a rich young nobleman, Franz von Schober, and struck up a lifetime's friendship with him. Schober gave Schubert a home, and later Schubert set his poetry to music. Apart from spending a couple of summers in Esterháza, working for relatives of Haydn's patron, he didn't travel much outside Vienna.

Schubert excelled at Lieder composition and wrote about 600 songs, encouraged by his friend, the singer Vogl. It is said that he could write six songs in one day. Some of the most famous of his settings are: the 'Erlking', the 'Trout', the 'Wanderer', and the song cycles: *Die Schöne Müllerin* and *Winterreise*. *Schwanengesang* is a group of songs collected after his death which are now performed as a cycle. Schubert invented the

Franz Schubert as a young man

*Winterreise*: Schubert said of these songs, 'They have taken more out of me than any other songs that I have written.' He called them, 'a bunch of terrifying songs'.

Schubert, seated at the piano, accompanies his friend Vogl at one of their frequent musical evenings

Schubert wrote a great deal of chamber music, but no concertos. In his chamber music – the *Death and the Maiden Quartet* and *The Trout Quintet*, for example – he used some of the melodies from his songs as themes for variations.

'song cycle' – a collection of separate songs to be performed together as a set. Schober set up musical evenings in his house, calling them 'Schubertiads', when only Schubert's music was played.

Schubert took his beautiful song melodies into the symphony. These simple tunes, full of child-like joy, often suddenly shift into the minor key, bringing a shadow across the music and hinting at the sadness of his life. By the time he was eighteen Schubert had written five symphonies, and wrote his last, the Ninth, when he was twenty-nine. He heard

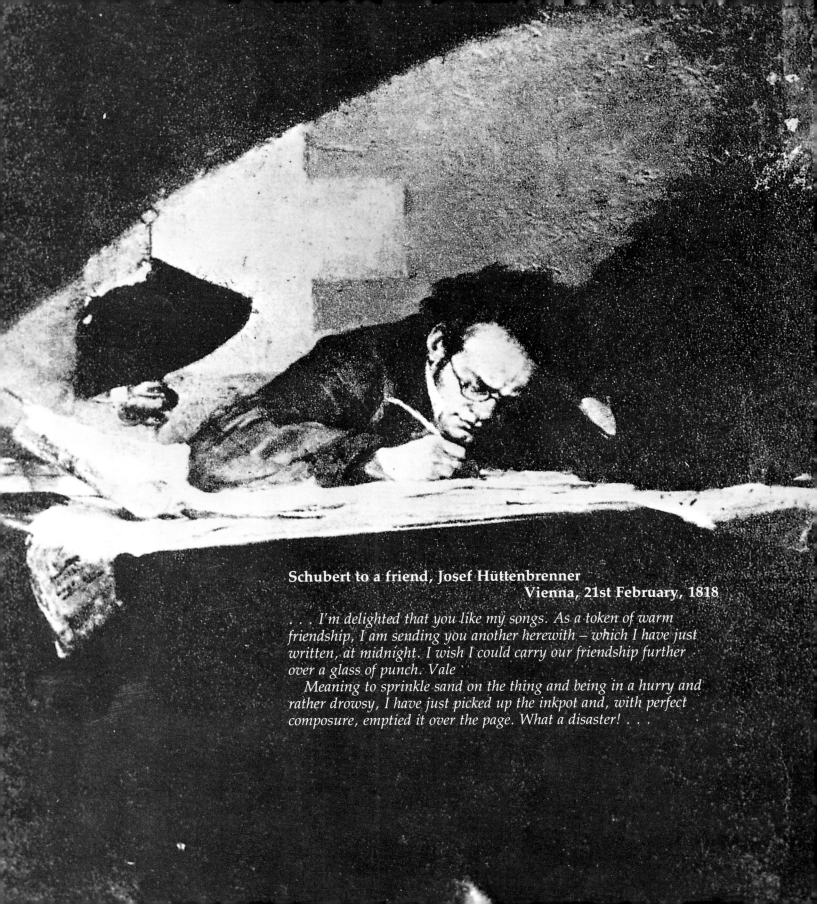

**Schubert to a friend, Josef Hüttenbrenner**
**Vienna, 21st February, 1818**

. . . I'm delighted that you like my songs. As a token of warm friendship, I am sending you another herewith – which I have just written, at midnight. I wish I could carry our friendship further over a glass of punch. Vale

Meaning to sprinkle sand on the thing and being in a hurry and rather drowsy, I have just picked up the inkpot and, with perfect composure, emptied it over the page. What a disaster! . . .

the Fifth – which was given a private performance in 1819 – but otherwise did not hear the others performed by an orchestra in his lifetime. The most famous symphonies are the last two – the Eighth, the 'Unfinished', and the Ninth, 'The Great C Major' – both of which were only discovered and performed after his death.

The Eighth is known as the 'Unfinished' because it consists of two movements and a sketch for the third. As it was written several years before his death, it is not known why he didn't finish it. He had taken composition classes with Antonio Salieri and became close friends with Anselm and Josef Hüttenbrenner of Graz. They idolised Schubert and arranged a commission for him. In 1822, he finally gave the unfinished work to Josef to pass on to Anselm and it went missing, turning up in a drawer forty years later. It was finally performed in Vienna in 1865, twenty-seven years after Schubert's death, and is usually thought of as the first truly Romantic symphony.

The Ninth, fifty minutes long, is in four movements, including a scherzo, and uses trombones. When Mendelssohn conducted the first performance several years after Schubert's death, the orchestra collapsed in giggles during the final movement. Since then, though, this movement has been described as having 'the momentum of a planet in its orbit'.

With Schubert's death came the end of what was later to be called the First Viennese School (Haydn, Mozart, Beethoven and Schubert) and therefore the end of an era. After this the musical centre of Europe shifted from Vienna. Two years after Schubert's death, Berlioz exploded on the scene in Paris with his Symphonie fantastique – a passionate outpouring of his own personal struggles with love.

Over the years, many compositions have been left unfinished by one composer and later finished by someone else. Mozart's *Requiem* was completed after his death by a pupil, Mahler's final symphony (No. 10), which originally consisted of one movement and a sketch of a second, is regularly performed as a two- or even three-movement work. Finishing these works is often achieved by someone in sympathy with the original composer, writing new music either based on sketches in notebooks left behind, or just through a general feel of how the music should sound.

# The Woodwind

The woodwind section of a modern symphony orchestra is made up of four different types of instrument: flutes, oboes, clarinets and bassoons, usually in pairs but sometimes doubled, making four of each, particularly in music for large orchestra from 1900 onwards. To this group may be added a piccolo (the highest flute), a cor anglais (lower oboe), bass clarinet (lowest clarinet) and double bassoon (lower bassoon) according to the requirements of the music. The composer usually states how many woodwind are required, although the decision to double the number may be taken by the conductor for reasons of balance and interpretation, according to the number of strings and other instruments.

In the modern orchestra, the woodwind sit behind the strings in the centre of the orchestra. The brass and percussion are behind them. Unlike the strings – where several instruments play one part – woodwind instruments have their own individual parts and are therefore 'soloists' in the orchestra. The first player of each section or group of instruments (the leader) plays the more important music, including any featured solo part.

It was discovered in ancient times that sounds could be made by blowing across one end of an animal bone, and that this sound could be varied by placing fingers over holes in the pipe and by changing the length of it.

The early woodwind instruments (shawms, flageolets, curtals, rackets) were difficult to play in tune and made a raucous sound. The early versions of the modern flutes, oboes, and bassoons were at first very simple in their construction and, although more tuneful, of limited range and versatility. This

Woodwind instruments are so-called because they were originally all made of wood. Modern instruments are made of wood, metal — including silver and gold — or plastic. They are divided into two types, depending on the shape of their bore, which is either cylindrical or conical.

made composers reluctant to give them individual parts in the orchestra – they were used mostly to copy the strings and add texture to the string sound. They were indispensable at this task, especially the oboes.

With the rise of instrumental music as an independent form, these instruments found they had a more important role. With the violin as lyrical soloist, composers and musicians would no longer suffer the unsophisticated woodwind sound. Louis XIV of France and Lully threw the woodwind out of the orchestra in disgust in the mid-1600s. Jean Hotteterre, a wind player in Louis XIV's orchestra, took on the task of improving the wind instruments, with the help of Michel Philidor, so they could make more pleasing sounds.

By the mid-1700s there is occasional reference to tunefulness of the woodwind in composers' letters and concert reviews. When the Mannheim Court Orchestra was established in 1741, a full woodwind group was used, including clarinets, which were then a new instrument in the orchestra. The better the woodwind sounded, the more music was written for them, until they achieved the sophisticated sounds and complex mechanism of modern instruments.

The flute has been around for a long time. Its use can be traced back to China in 9 BC. It arrived in Germany from Byzantium in the twelfth century and from there it spread through Europe, establishing itself in England after 1500. Much of its popularity is owed to the favour it found with royalty – Henry VIII, for instance, not only played the flute but had a large number that formed part of his collection of strange and bizarre musical instruments. His flutes were made of various materials – wood, glass and silver, and consisted of a single pipe with six fingerholes.

The flute was first used in the orchestra by Lully for the

*'The flute is not an instrument which has a good moral effect. It is too exciting.'*

Aristotle

Frederick the Great of Prussia, a
virtuoso flautist, playing at court

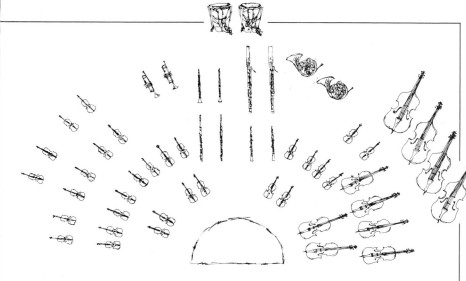

A typical layout of an orchestra
when performing a Classical work
today

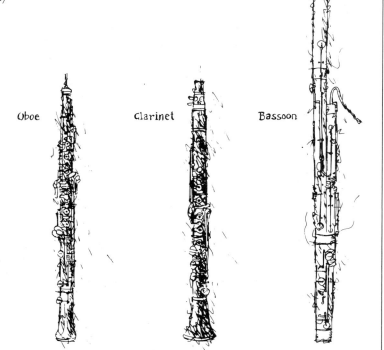

Oboe

Clarinet

Bassoon

Piccolo

Flute

performance of a ballet at Louis xiv's court in 1681. King Frederick the Great of Prussia played flute concertos every evening to his courtiers. He also composed a great deal of difficult music for the instrument, which is still played today. In addition, the court composer, Quantz, wrote over 300 flute concertos for the king, as well as an *Essay of a Method for Playing the Transverse Flute* (1752). By the late eighteenth century, the flute had overtaken the recorder in popularity.

The most significant improvement to the flute was made in 1831 when Theobald Boehm, a goldsmith, jeweller and flautist from Munich, designed a new system of keys. Holes that were previously difficult to reach with the fingers could now be played easily with the sixteen keys moving at the slightest touch. In 1843, Berlioz wrote in his *Treatise on Orchestration* that the flute, 'has now achieved such perfection and evenness of tone that no further improvement remains to be desired'.

The modern flute comes in three parts, or joints – the foot, body and head. Its lowest note is normally Middle C, its highest the C three octaves above, although a skilled player can extend this range, and play a little higher.

The piccolo is a miniature flute and plays higher notes – in fact, the highest in the orchestra. It first appeared in the orchestra in the eighteenth century. It too had the Boehm key system added to it and is played in the same way as the flute. Sitting in the orchestra as part of the woodwind section, the piccolo player is at the end of a long row of instruments, and often has very little to play. Consequently, the second flautist sometimes doubles on the piccolo.

The name oboe comes from the French *hautbois*, meaning 'high wood'. The instrument was originally made of boxwood and was very simple, with only two or three keys.

Reed instruments, from which the oboe descended, are

The Latin word *tibia* means 'flute' and 'shin bone', which indicates the origins of the instrument. The name 'flute' comes from the Latin *flatus*, meaning 'breath' or 'blowing'.

Playing the flute is like blowing across the top of a bottle. As with all wind instruments, controlling the breath is vital for good sound production; a player must learn not only how to blow smoothly to produce an even tone, but also how to vary the speed with which the air is blown because this changes not only the pitch of the note, but also determines whether, for example, a middle G or high G is played, since the same keys are pressed for both notes.

Players often invent their own devices to feel secure when performing. With a flute, for example, a piece of sticking plaster under the mouthpiece resting on the chin will stop the instrument from slipping if the player perspires.

The oboe's sound is produced by blowing through a double reed – two flat reeds bound together. Players usually make their own reeds as they are crucial to the sound and must be exactly the right thickness. The reed must be wet in order to vibrate and make a sound. A player can check it by blowing it before putting it in the instrument, making sure it produces a thick, squawking sound. While the reed must be wet, the instrument itself must be dry inside – if water finds its way into the instrument it becomes unplayable.

much older than the flute. They date from the third millennium BC, the Greek aulos being one of the earliest double reed instruments. In the Middle Ages, the English used the shawm, based on the Eastern instrument, the zurna, which had been used to frighten off the Crusaders.

The oboe found its way into the orchestra, like the flute, through the work of Hotteterre. It quickly became very popular, especially in England. French players were imported to play it and Henry Purcell used it in his instrumental music during the seventeenth century. At this time there were several different sizes of instrument in use, including the oboe d'amore and oboe da caccia. Purcell used a 'tenor oboe' which is now, as a result, known as the English horn (cor anglais). In a modern orchestra only one type of oboe is used regularly – the cor anglais and oboe d'amore are added only if the piece demands it.

Various important craftsmen have contributed to the oboe's development over the centuries: Louis Buffet applied the Boehm mechanism in 1844 but the French didn't like the new sound at first. Both the French and Germans make oboes very successfully. To the trained ear there is a distinct difference between the two sounds, and endless debate as to which sounds better.

The oboe is the highest of the reed instruments and looks very much like a clarinet. It is most easily recognised by the slender reed at the top – the clarinet, by comparison, has a solid mouthpiece with a single reed. The top notes on an oboe are difficult to reach and can sound thin and precarious, but it does have a plaintive quality that is very good for melancholy tunes. It can also be used to chirp like a bird.

The clarinet is a member of the single reed family. Its early ancestors were the hornpipe and various kinds of bagpipe. By the late 1600s the chalumeau had appeared, from which the modern clarinet was later developed.

The word clarinet means 'little clarino' (little trumpet), and the early ones had a trumpet-like sound. The instrument arrived late in the orchestra compared with other wind instruments, invented by J.C. Denner of Nuremberg in the late 1600s. Denner died before his instrument was used regularly, although it was taken up by composers as soon as it appeared. Vivaldi wrote three clarinet concertos towards the end of his life. Records show that a clarinet concerto was played in Dublin in 1742. In 1789 the Stadler brothers, Mozart's billiard partners, added extra keys and introduced the instrument to the composer. To Mozart, the clarinet seemed to resemble the voice more than any other instrument – it is easy to imagine that he was thinking of the soprano voice when he composed his Clarinet Concerto.

The clarinet comes in several sizes and tunings – the E flat is the smallest and plays the highest notes, followed by the B flat, the A and the bass. It is a 'transposing instrument', which means that the notes played are different from those the player reads on the score. It has two registers – the lower one is known as the chalumeau register. The point where the tone changes to the high register is called the 'break' and great skill is required to play evenly over it.

Bassoon means 'big bass'. The instrument developed from

To blow on the reed, a player wraps his lips over his teeth and places the reed between them, taking care not to break the reed's tip. He then blows very hard, using the diaphragm to control the air and push it through the reed, and using the muscles in the corners of the mouth to hold the reed in position. After many hours playing, it is possible that these muscles get tired. Players complain 'my lip has gone', meaning that they can no longer grip the reed. This is a common problem for beginners until the lip muscles strengthen.

Blowing the clarinet is similar to the oboe in that it requires breath control. But the clarinet can start at silence and get louder and louder, then softer and softer, ending in silence.

Berlioz wrote some interesting tips about how to write for the clarinet. At the end of the March to the Scaffold (Symphonie fantastique) a theme is played on the clarinet and demonstrates Berlioz's advice:

*The entry of the clarinet should be hidden under a strong chord of the entire orchestra until the tone has come firm and clear.*

The bassoon literature started with Vivaldi, who wrote thirty-nine solo concertos for it. Stravinsky, in 1913, starts *The Rite of Spring* with a bassoon solo, using it at the top of its range. He did this deliberately because he wanted it to strive to reach a note beyond its range and, in doing so, gives the sound a quality of struggle.

the curtal, this name meaning something which is shortened by being folded. The Italian name for the instrument is fagotto, meaning 'bundle of sticks'.

The bassoon, like the oboe, is a double reed instrument. Its role in the woodwind section is to play 'bass oboe'. Two instruments are commonly used – the bassoon and the contrabassoon, both of which are made of lengths of wooden tubing curled round into a convenient shape. The bassoon is eight and a half feet long, the contrabassoon sixteen feet. When played, they are supported on a sling round the player's neck.

Usually made of maple, the bassoon came into its own when the German instrument maker, Heckel, designed a key system for it which made it more flexible. This is the system still commonly used today. The bassoon is the only wind instrument with keys to be played by the thumbs – they have to be able to cover nine keys altogether. It has a range of three and a half octaves – the biggest of all woodwind instruments. The contrabassoon competes with the tuba to play the lowest notes in the orchestra.

The bassoon is good at wide leaps and can make comic sounds, which give it the reputation of being the clown of the orchestra. But it also blends well with other instruments – in the overture to Mozart's *Marriage of Figaro* there is a difficult solo bassoon part played against the main string theme, which adds a special colour to the overall sound.

# The Romantics

## 1828-1910

Romantic composers believed that the prime function of music was to express emotion, making all other criteria subservient to this aim. The orchestra grew in size: brass were used as a regular section in the orchestra more frequently, and composers poured out their most personal feelings about love and life in their music. The symphony, established in the Classical Era by Haydn, Mozart, Beethoven and Schubert, experienced its most glorious hundred years.

*'Music should be the direct reaction to emotion.'*

Hector Berlioz

After the French Revolution, the idea of the freedom of the individual became increasingly important. Beethoven expressed this in his opera *Fidelio*, when Florestan is finally released after years of captivity in a dungeon under the ground. As the expression of personal feelings became more acceptable in society, so music and art reflected this new sense of freedom. The imagination ran riot, with composers, writers and artists living out the dream of the artist as romantic hero, openly suffering in the name of art, only to die, young and desperate. With this came the need to reveal the nightmare side of human existence – fear of the Devil, corruption, and the sinister side of life, as expressed in Goethe's (1749–1832) story of Faust, who traded his soul with the Devil in return for immortality and the promise of eternal love.

Music history books were being written, organising music into periods – Baroque and Classical – and drawing attention to the works of the great masters who had gone before, contributing to a new reverence for composers and orchestral music.

Musical life included chamber music at home, public orchestral concerts in concert halls, and large-scale opera productions. Composers worked more and more on a freelance basis, composing by commission. They were no longer servants in a household, but placed themselves on pedestals to be respected and revered. Even so, they still often suffered from lack of recognition and, although they could become rich and famous, the freelance life was then, as it is now, quite precarious. They continued to travel more, working in other countries – moving towards the international lifestyle of orchestral musicians today. Composers came into contact with each other more often, conducting or performing each other's work. They gave opinions about each other's music, mostly

The harp is one of the oldest instruments, dating back to 1200 BC. It was only from 1810, when Sebastian Erard invented the pedal harp, making it more versatile, that it became a useful orchestral instrument. It has forty-seven strings, some coloured red and others blue to help the player identify them. The word harp comes from the Latin *arpa*, meaning 'spread-out chords'. The pedals enable the player to change quickly to other keys. It takes at least half an hour to tune, so the poor harpist is always first on the concert platform.

in support but sometimes quite ungenerous, and vicious.

*'Berlioz is a regular freak without a vestige of talent.'*

Rossini

*'Such an astounding lack of talent was never before united to such pretentiousness.'*

Tchaikovksy on Strauss

**Promenade Concerts.**
It was Queen Victoria and Prince Albert who started the fashion for Promenade Concerts in London in 1840. They both loved music and wanted to encourage public interest in it. Seasons of concerts, following the fashion in France, sprang up in several London theatres around this time.

The cor anglais makes low, melancholy notes, which are deeply expressive. Dvořák uses it beautifully in the 'New World' Symphony, playing a melody inspired by Minnehaha's funeral in *Hiawatha*.

The saxophone was invented by Adolphe Sax in Paris in 1840. Although made of brass, it is actually classified as a woodwind instrument as it is shaped like a bass clarinet and has a single reed mouthpiece. Only used occasionally in orchestral music, it is a popular jazz instrument.

The increase in public concerts encouraged the enlargement of the orchestra to a much grander scale, until it became almost larger than life, using a brass section on a regular basis, more woodwind, and additional instruments, such as harps and the piano. Brass instruments at this time were liberated by the invention of the valve in about 1818, making them more flexible and easier to play.

Composers found this enlarged orchestra the perfect vehicle to express their personal feelings. Tone colour was a very important ingredient of this, making the individual timbres of instruments all the more significant. Additional instruments were added for their special sounds. To the staple woodwind section of flutes, oboes, clarinets and bassoons, were added piccolo, cor anglais, E flat clarinet, bass clarinet, saxophone, contrabassoon, and existing instruments were much improved. Instrument makers had raised the pitch of woodwind instruments to make them sound more exciting. This in turn made problems for the brass, which had to be adapted accordingly to stay in tune with them.

Although the pedal harp was available, it was often difficult to get a good player, so the harp part was often played on the piano instead. The string section remained the same. The violin and viola acquired chin rests from about 1820, making

The first Handel Festival at Crystal Palace in 1859

them more comfortable to play. The percussion section increased from the Classical use of two kettledrums, to three or more. With the growing fascination for Turkish music came little drums, cymbals and the triangle.

It became fashionable to give concerts with huge orchestras. In 1800 an orchestra totalling forty players would have been normal. By 1880, the strings alone would number that, having become more numerous to keep pace with the burgeoning woodwind and brass. These changes meant that the orchestra could regularly number over a hundred players, although the concept of the four basic sections continued – strings, woodwind, brass and percussion.

Because of the fashion for big orchestras, earlier works were also performed using many more instruments than originally intended. For example, the conductor Spohr performed Haydn's oratorio *The Seasons* in St Petersburg (*c.*1802) with

The idea of giving concerts with huge orchestras was not new. The Handel Commemoration in 1784 used 250 instruments and 275 voices in Westminster Abbey. In 1786, *Messiah* was performed in Berlin Cathedral with an orchestra of 189 and a chorus of 119. This practice continued for festive occasions. Jullien conducted concerts of Haydn and Beethoven in the Surrey Zoological Gardens with an orchestra of 300 players. In 1859 he conducted *Messiah* in the same place with an orchestra and chorus totalling 1,000.

seventy violins, thirty double basses and doubling of all wood-wind. This practice continued well into the twentieth century, only recently changing with the current fashion for 'authentic' performance.

Festivals were an opportunity to push the boat out and present music on a gigantic scale. Berlioz wanted to present, as he put it, 'monster' music. He believed that music with the 'breadth of style' of the oratorios of Handel, Bach, Haydn and Beethoven, 'no doubt have much to gain from performances by larger forces'. Always campaigning for more players, he believed that the importance of a large orchestra was not only for its volume, but also for its power. Large sounds and strong textures were essential to express the swirling emotions of Romanticism. Venues for these large-scale concerts were all important. In Berlioz's case, if the hall wasn't big enough, the orchestra would simply play outside. Composers generally became fanatical about the positioning of players for perform-ances and there were many different theories about correct placing and balance of sound. Even today, the layout of the symphony orchestra can vary according to the requirements of the music or the composer's or conductor's personal prefer-ence.

As the orchestra grew larger, the music it played became longer. Beethoven had already upset critics with his 'Eroica' Symphony (1803) because it was forty minutes long. By the nineteenth century composers like Bruckner and Mahler were writing symphonies of over an hour in length – in Mahler's case the longest being one hour forty-five minutes (the Eighth), adding voices like an operatic composition. Wagner, in turn, wrote his operas 'symphonically', the longest of which is *The Ring*, which is in four separate parts totalling eighteen hours.

Berlioz conducted a concert in 1844 to close the Exhibition of Industrial Products. He employed every orchestral player and singer that he could find in Paris. He rehearsed the (as he put it), 'body of 1,022 performers' in sections. In one session he had thirty-six double basses playing the scherzo from Beethoven's Fifth Symphony and remarked that they sounded like 'the grunting of a herd of stampeding pigs, the playing was so ragged and out of tune'. But, fortunately, they got better with practice!

II.—DRAWING-ROOM MUSIC OF THE PRESENT—A BRILLIANT FANTASIA FOR THE PIANO BY SIGNOR RUMBELSTOMSKINI.

Cartoon from *Punch* satirising the popular salon concerts

*A tone poem or symphonic poem*: a piece of orchestral music in one continuous movement based on a programme or story, usually a poetic text which is meant to be read by the audience before listening to the music. Liszt coined the term 'symphonic poem', Strauss the term 'tone poem'.

*Theme*: a musical idea, usually a melody, which forms the basis or starting point of a musical composition. It can also be called a 'subject'.

Alongside this obsession with hugeness there was also a miniature approach. Salon music was still very fashionable, with private performances by leading composers such as Chopin, who wrote hundreds of solo piano compositions for this purpose.

Romantic composers lost their deference to the ordered structures set up in the Classical period. Some broke the rules inside the school grounds (Beethoven, Schubert, Mendelssohn, Schumann, Brahms), while others climbed over the walls (Berlioz, Liszt, Wagner, Bruckner, Mahler and Strauss), creating a new form of descriptive music which would tell a story, following all its extreme moods and passions. Out of this grew the musical form the tone poem, or symphonic poem, which was a descriptive symphony performed in one continuous movement.

Another feature of Romantic music was to use themes to convey a character or mood, revealing the character's feelings by changing the context in which the themes appear. Carl

Maria von Weber (1786–1826) (the cousin of Mozart's wife) started doing this in his opera *Der Freischütz* in 1821.

In 1830, only two years after Schubert's death, Hector Berlioz (1803–69) exploded onto the Romantic scene with his Symphonie fantastique – a passionate outpouring of his own personal struggles with love. It was first performed using a large orchestra of about 120 players (he had hoped for 220), including harps, E flat clarinet, cornets, two tubas and piano. He uses a large brass section and gives them important themes to perform. The piece is fifty-five minutes in length. Berlioz was the ultimate Romantic, struggling with unrequited love. Throughout his life he dreamt of one chance to use his ideal orchestra of 465 players, including 30 pianos and 30 harps. His music was not admired by everyone and, like his life, is very tempestuous.

In the Symphonie fantastique Berlioz uses a theme (*idée fixe*) to portray his love, Harriet. One of the five movements describes how he imagines he is being marched to the scaffold. We hear the guillotine drop at the end, and the 'plink plonk' as the head falls. Just before this, a solo clarinet plays Harriet's theme, the *idée fixe*, as he thinks of her before he dies. Berlioz also wrote volumes of literary works and enjoyed making highly exaggerated emotional declarations:

If I were rich, very rich, I would go to Mehemet-Ali, or the Sultan, and I would say: 'Highness, sell the island of Tenedos, sell me Cape Sigeium and Simois and Scamander. Don't be alarmed – it has nothing to do with the war. Once I had become master of those places consecrated by the Muse of Antiquity, of those hills, those woods where flowed the blood of Hector and the tears of Andromache, I would fit out a vessel and embark a great orchestra, and set sail for Troy. When I

*Right above* Hector Berlioz: 'My life is a deeply interesting romance'

*Right below* Harriet Smithson, with whom the composer fell passionately in love

Poulenc wrote a chorus for nuns (for his opera, *The Carmelites*) waiting to be guillotined. As each head is chopped off, one by one, a dull thud is heard and the number of voices decreases until there is only one voice left – and then none!

Berlioz wrote that his ideal orchestra for a hall scarcely larger than the Paris Conservatory would be: 41 violins, 18 violas, 8 first cellos, 7 second cellos, 10 double basses, 4 harps, 2 piccolos, 2 flutes, 1 English horn, 2 clarinets, 1 basset horn or bass clarinet, 4 bassoons, 4 valve horns, 2 valve trumpets, 2 piston cornets, 3 trombones, 1 bass trombone, 1 bass tuba, 2 pairs of timpani with 4 drummers, 1 bass drum and 1 pair of cymbals – 119 players. To this he would add a chorus of 126, and if the size of the hall could cope he would DOUBLE THESE NUMBERS.

Berlioz was born into a prosperous family. His father was a skilled surgeon and wanted Hector to study medicine too. Berlioz says in his *Memoirs*, 'Love and music were revealed to me at the age of twelve.' This was his first love, Estelle. Later, frustrated that Harriet Smithson wouldn't return his affections, he was seduced by Camille Moke and became engaged to her. Having won the coveted Prix de Rome, he went off to Italy to study. During this time she was unfaithful to him. Hearing that Camille was to marry someone else, he decided to kill her, her lover and her mother. Imagining his revenge, he went into a milliner's and asked for a complete lady's maid outfit, as a disguise. He reports: 'I ceremonially loaded a pair of double-barrelled pistols which I had with me, examined and replaced in my pocket two small bottles of those invaluable cordials, laudanum and strychnine.' He set out to find the trio, intent on murder. In the event he lost his lady's outfit, the police stopped him because they thought he was a revolutionary, and finally, realising that if he carried out the deed he would have to kill himself also, he concluded that he could not 'say farewell to life and art, and leave behind me the reputation of a boor, a savage who did not know how to live, to leave my symphony unfinished,' and changed his mind. 'Work and art are the two sovereign remedies for an afflicted mind.'

arrived in that sublime country I would create a place of solitude. No more Italian amateurs, no English tourists . . . I would build a temple of sound at the foot of Mount Ida, and there, one evening, my royal orchestra should recite that other poem by the king of musicians, the Eroica Symphony of Beethoven.'

Berlioz fell in love with the Irish Shakespearean actress, Harriet Smithson, but it is hardly surprising that, although they eventually married, she resisted his advances for some time. He would overwhelm her with his love, once even lying down in the road in front of her carriage in desperation to get her attention. On one occasion he apparently said to her, 'I am your slave,' to which she replied, 'Slavery has been abolished!' He was fascinated by the romantic aspects of Shakespeare, so it was no accident that he fell in love with her when she was playing Ophelia in *Hamlet*.

Berlioz wrote a *Treatise on Orchestration* (1843), a bible of musical instruments in which he describes each one in loving detail, explaining their strengths and weaknesses and how best to exploit their sounds in the orchestra. Richard Strauss later revised the book, adding a section about conducting.

In his scores, Berlioz gives exact instructions about instruments and how they should be played, aiming to display the individual glory of each one. He gives the brass important themes to play instead of just using them to reinforce a climax. The *Requiem* is scored for about 200 players, including four satellite brass choirs at each corner of the platform. Space permitting, he would use a chorus of 400 singers for this work. He understood dramatic 'staging' of his music and his orchestral sound is always distinctive.

Unfortunately, he often wasn't taken seriously because he

The violinist Paganini, a committed supporter of Berlioz's music, returned to Paris to hear Berlioz's opera *Benvenuto Cellini* which was not successful. Berlioz himself said, 'They savaged it.' A few days later Berlioz received a note from Paganini enclosing 20,000 francs. The note read: 'Beethoven being dead, only Berlioz can make him live again.' Berlioz went to thank Paganini, finding him eventually in a nearby tavern, playing billiards.

was so outrageous. Cartoons showed him conducting with a sword. For many years he struggled with financial problems and his opera productions were relatively unsuccessful. Like Schumann, he earned a living as a music critic, and also wrote his *Memoirs*, which are a fascinating and dramatic account of his life and relationship to other musicians of his generation.

It was becoming more and more usual for a composer to earn a living by conducting. With orchestras and concert societies springing up all over Europe, there was competition for the best positions.

Felix Mendelssohn Bartholdy (1809–47) was conductor of the Leipzig Gewandhaus Orchestra for most of his life. Son of a rich Hamburg banker, he had composed thirteen string symphonies, an opera, a string octet and the overture to *A Midsummer Night's Dream* (1827) by the age of seventeen – works of surprising maturity and perfection of form. Coming from a rich family, he never had any money problems, which in turn caused him to be the victim of jealousy and resentment at times. His Songs Without Words for the piano are known by all pianists. He did a great deal to promote the work of past composers, starting in 1829 at the age of twenty by conducting the first performance in the nineteenth century of Bach's *St Matthew Passion*, a century after the first performance by Bach himself. He used a large orchestra for this – over seventy players – and a chorus of 400 singers. Later he revived many of Handel's oratorios, forgotten works of Mozart, Beethoven sym-

*Below* Felix Mendelssohn Bartholdy

phonies (especially the Ninth) and Schubert's Great C Major Symphony.

Mendelssohn's symphonies stay within the Classical framework of four movements and are about twenty-five minutes in duration. He adds a programme element to his *Hebrides* overture 'Fingal's Cave'. 'In order to make you understand how inordinately the Hebrides have affected me I have written down the following which comes into my mind,' he wrote to his family on 7 August 1829 after taking the steamer from Fort William to Oban and from Oban to Tobermory, seeing Fingal's Cave on the Isle of Staffa. The effect of the storm in this overture is remarkable considering he did not use anything larger than the Classical-size orchestra.

After conducting 'Fingal's Cave' in London in 1832 he revised it on the grounds that: 'The so-called development smacks more of counterpoint than of oil and seagulls and dead fish – it should be just the opposite.'

Mendelssohn conducted Schumann's First Symphony in 1841. Robert Schumann (1810–56) also stayed within the Classical framework, but used the trombones to play tunes as well as fill in the harmony. He also uses three kettledrums instead of the usual Classical two, and in his Spring Symphony follows Beethoven in his use of pastoral ideas, using horn calls and the solo flute for the last signs of spring. Like Beethoven, he also uses the scherzo in place of the minuet. He wrote four symphonies, which are large-scale works in four movements, each about thirty minutes long. He also wrote a piano and a cello concerto, piano miniatures, and song cycles. His friend, the composer and pianist Franz Liszt, performed a lot of his music.

Franz (Ferenc) Liszt (1811–86) was known for his extraordinary virtuoso piano technique. A multi-talented musician, he

**Mendelssohn's letter to his mother**
Prince Albert asked me to go to him on Saturday so that I might try his organ before I left England. Queen Victoria came in while we were talking. She asked if I had written any new songs, and said she was very fond of singing my published ones. Prince Albert went off to find some music. I begged her to sing one of my first sets of songs, and she did – in strict time and tune, and with very good execution.

One evening, whilst having supper with the Schumanns, Liszt made some snide remarks about Mendelssohn. Schumann immediately arose, seized Liszt by the shoulder and cried, 'How dare you talk like that about our great Mendelssohn.' Liszt apologised and left.

played the March to the Scaffold from Berlioz's Symphonie fantastique on the piano and seemingly made it sound more dramatic than the full orchestral version. He called Berlioz 'an adventurer' and 'terror of the Philistines'. Apart from being one of the most sought-after pianists of his day, he was also a talented conductor, giving the first performance of several Wagner operas. They knew each other well – Wagner married Liszt's daughter, Cosima.

As a composer Liszt pioneered the symphonic poem. His most productive years were from 1848, when he settled in Weimar as Musical Director, with an orchestra and a theatre at his disposal, although it's said the orchestra here was quite small.

His symphonic poems are in one, highly descriptive movement, and, like Berlioz's, use one theme to represent a character. He wrote the often gruesome details of the story in the front of the score. They are based on subjects such as *Hamlet*, Goethe's play *Tasso* and *The Slaughter of the Huns*. Later he wrote programme symphonies, the first being 'Faust', which is in three movements and copies the ideas of Berlioz again, expressing the development of the characters through the music.

Johannes Brahms (1833–97) another composer-pianist, and great friend of Schumann, made Vienna his home from the age of thirty. A very talented pianist, living in Vienna at a time when Beethoven's symphonies were very popular (1863), Brahms felt he was living in Beethoven's shadow. Consequently he didn't write his first symphony until he was forty-three years old. The breakthrough for him came in 1873 when he orchestrated his piano duet Variations on a Theme of Joseph Haydn, the 'St Antony Chorale'. He uses a very simple orchestra, without trombones, and, as the piece was well

*'Beethoven attended Liszt's concert in 1823 (when Liszt was twelve years old). Seeing Beethoven in the front row unnerved rather than staggered him. Amid the storm of applause at the end, Beethoven (who of course was deaf by then) stepped on the platform, took Liszt in his arms and kissed him on both cheeks.'*
Revd Hugh Reginald Hawes, *My Musical Life*, 1854

*Below* Franz Liszt

Brahms played in taverns in the dock area of Hamburg as a small boy with his father, who was a double bass player. He gave his first solo recital in 1848 when he was fifteen years old. In 1860, he signed a manifesto against Liszt's new styles of composition, which is one of the reasons why (as Liszt was close to Wagner) he was thought to be anti-Wagner.

Robert Schumann died when Brahms was twenty-three years old, and Brahms remained friends with Clara, secretly in love with her all his life.

Three years before he wrote his First Symphony, he composed a set of variations for two pianos based on a theme he borrowed from Haydn. Clara Schumann and he played the piece at its first performance in a private house in Bonn in 1873.

Johannes Brahms

received, it encouraged him to continue with orchestral writing.

His First Symphony (1876) is in four movements, is forty-six minutes in duration and uses a theme similar to the 'joy' melody in the last movement of Beethoven's Ninth Symphony. When challenged about this he remarked, 'Anyone can see that.' Like Beethoven, he also uses a double bassoon and three trombones, which, also like Beethoven, are only used in the last movement of the symphony.

After this he wrote three more symphonies, two concertos for piano, one for violin, one for violin and cello and overtures, choral works and many songs. His symphonies used the traditional four-movement pattern, but he didn't give them descriptive titles, although in his third symphony he uses a motto – the musical notes F A F, meaning 'Frei aber Froh' (Free but Happy).

The pianist-conductor, Hans von Bülow, performed Brahms's piano music. His wife, (Liszt's daughter) Cosima, left him and married Wagner. Von Bülow, naturally upset, no longer wished to support Wagner's music, and instead took to championing Brahms (who was seen as a rival of Wagner) taking him and his symphonies on tour with the prestigious Meiningen Orchestra, which was a great encouragement to Brahms.

Whilst rehearsing Brahms's Fourth and final Symphony (the only one Brahms conducted himself), von Bülow took on the young Richard Strauss as Assistant Conductor. He called Wagner 'Richard the First' and Strauss, 'Richard the Third' – after Wagner there could be no second.

Richard Strauss (1864–1949) – no relation to the family who wrote Viennese waltzes – was a composer-conductor, holding positions in opera houses in Munich, Weimar, Berlin

Joachim, the violinist, was a great friend of Brahms and Schumann. Schumann proposed that they should compose a violin sonata for Joachim and let him guess the author of each movement. Clara Schumann accompanied Joachim on the piano, and he immediately recognised who had written each part. Schumann dedicated it to Joachim, using Joachim's motto, which was *Frei Aber Einsam* (Free But Lonely).

Brahms and Wagner represented two conflicting schools of German Romantic music and for this reason people thought them to be enemies. This is not true. Brahms was fascinated by Wagner's music and, although he never went to Bayreuth, he offered to copy parts of *Die Meistersinger* in Vienna in 1863 just to work with him.

and Vienna. Another child genius, Strauss was the son of one of the finest horn players in Germany. He composed from the age of five, when he wrote a polka and Christmas carol. His father was principal horn player with the Munich Court Opera and it was by accompanying him to work that the young Strauss heard all the major operatic works of the time, including Wagner's *Tannhäuser* and *Siegfried*. Strauss's verdict at the time was that he found them totally boring. He did, however, go on to study Wagner's scores as a student and, when he started work for von Bülow and the Meiningen Orchestra, he met Alexander Ritter and other Wagner fanatics, who converted him to the cause. He spent time in Bayreuth, Wagner's opera house, as a repetiteur (rehearsal pianist).

He came to conducting by chance when Hans von Bülow, who had commissioned Strauss in 1884 to write a suite for wind instruments for the Meiningen Orchestra, made him conduct the first performance in Munich at short notice, having never held a baton in his life. He was twenty years old.

Despite his childhood reaction to Wagner's music, the composer was later to influence Strauss's compositions because it was after hearing Wagner's music that he began to write programme music in the form of tone poems. Strauss wrote eleven in ten years, the first of which, *Don Juan*, was completed in 1889 when he was twenty-five years old. These tone poems mark the start of his enormous success as an orchestral storyteller. They were played all over Europe and the USA. In each he takes an imagined hero as the central character, for instance Don Juan (1889), Till Eulenspiegel (1895) and Don Quixote (1897). Each character in the story is represented by a theme which Strauss weaves throughout the music.

Acclaim for Strauss's work was not unanimous, though. Debussy described *Till Eulenspiegel* as 'an hour of original music in a lunatic asylum'. The US newspaper headline after the premiere of *Salomé* in 1905 read, '4000 survive the most appalling tragedy ever shown on the stage.' Strauss himself was convinced that *Don Juan* was going to be a flop. During the rehearsals he wrote to his father, saying 'I feel very sorry for the poor horns and trumpets – they blew until they were blue in the face.' But the first performance in Weimar on 11 November 1889 was a great success and marked the start of an international career during which he was to write orchestral, chamber and piano music, operas, concertos and around 200 songs.

In 1903 he wrote an autobiographical symphony, the Symphonia Domestica and then turned to writing operas. *Salomé* (1905) and *Elektra* (1909) are highly charged, intensely emotional operas which must have been extremely shocking when first performed. His music, especially for *Elektra*, pushed

In 1948 in Munich Sir Georg Solti conducted Strauss's opera *Der Rosenkavalier* for the composer's eighty-fifth birthday. He reports their first meeting:

*'He (Strauss) came to the dress rehearsal of* Rosenkavalier. *It was the first time I had conducted it and I was very nervous about him being there. He said nice things about it and invited me to his home. So I went, taking with me all my Strauss opera scores, hoping to pick up some first-hand information. Although I was terrified of him, he immediately put me at ease. I learnt more in that one morning about opera conducting than the whole of my life up to that point.'*

'Strauss told me that when you are rehearsing opera you must always move away from the orchestra and listen to the sound in the auditorium because it sounds totally different out there. Since then I have never done an opera without doing this.'

Sir Georg Solti

*Left* Peter Ilyich Tchaikovsky

Anton Rubinstein, Tchaikovsky's teacher, spoke of Tchaikovsky's ability to write music: 'Once in a composition class I set him an exercise to write contrapuntal variations on a given theme. I expected he'd write about a dozen. At the next class he gave me two hundred. It would have taken me longer to examine all these than he took to write them.'

Tchaikovsky wrote from Hamburg to his nephew: 'The conductor here is not merely passable but actually has genius and ardently desires to conduct the first performance of my opera *Eugene Onegin*. His name is Mahler. The singers, orchestra, manager of the theatre and Mahler all love *Onegin*; but I am very doubtful whether the Hamburg public will share their enthusiasm.'

harmony to its limits. He is reported as saying about it: 'I went to the edge of the cliff and looked down the precipice and I was horrified – I had to go back.' He was afraid what the music of the future might hold, and turned back to a lush, Romantic style to write *Der Rosenkavalier*. As he was dying, he wrote the exquisite *Four Last Songs* for soprano and orchestra – an outstanding tribute to his life's work.

Peter Ilyich Tchaikovsky (1840–93), another composer – pianist, was one of the most important symphonists outside the German/Austrian tradition. His many orchestral works include six symphonies with varying numbers of movements, two piano concertos, a violin concerto, the Rococo Variations for cello, and many overtures – most famously the *1812 Overture*.

The first three symphonies and the sixth have names. The fourth is autobiographical, scored for large orchestra with trombones, tuba, bass drum, symbols and triangle. The subject is 'Fate' – 'the fatal power which prevents our striving for happiness from succeeding'. The mood of his music swings through a wide emotional range, from frenzied happiness to utter gloom.

The late Romantics pushed emotional expression to the limits, bringing in elements of personal hopelessness and despair. Music was losing its optimism. Gustav Mahler (1860–1911) shows this particularly. One moment one is dancing a light-hearted *Ländler* (German peasant dance) through the mountains of Austria with no cares in the world. The next moment, suicidal despair. Mahler became great friends with Richard Strauss and, like him, made a living by conducting operas.

His life was full of tragedy and he was terrified that his music was in some way a premonition of the future. He wasn't wrong to think this. For example, Rückert wrote some poems on the death of his children which Mahler then set to music in 1904 (*Kindertotenlieder*). Soon after, one of Mahler's own daughters died, and he never forgave himself, thinking that he had in some way tempted fate by writing the music. In the same year he was diagnosed as having heart disease. There was a superstition that composers died after writing nine symphonies, as Beethoven, Schubert and Bruckner had done. Mahler tried to delay writing his Ninth Symphony by writing *Das Lied von der Erde*, a set of orchestral songs, thinking of them as, but not calling them, his Ninth Symphony. Ironically, he did not outwit his destiny, dying before completing his Tenth.

Mahler was a master of colossal orchestration but, as well as creating huge landscapes of sound, his music can suddenly become simple and child-like, evoking his childhood memories. Although he mostly uses traditional instruments,

Mahler was a great friend of Bruckner and conducted all his symphonies in New York. He recalls a story about Bruckner: 'After an illness Bruckner was ordered by his doctor to take a daily hip bath. He would compose while in the tub. While absorbed in his work one day, the mother of one of his pupils knocked on the door. "Come in," called Bruckner. He jumped out of the tub and went over to greet her, forgetting that he was totally naked. She shrieked and ran out. And this had to happen to Bruckner, who blushed like a schoolboy if he so much as looked at a woman.'

Mahler occasionally adds unusual ones to create a special effect – sleigh bells in the Fourth Symphony, mandolin in the Seventh and Eighth. He was the first to start a symphony in one key and finish it in another – meaning the music does not return to the home key.

His First Symphony (1888) was written as a symphonic poem but he later changed it because he disliked the descriptive titles. Now in four movements, it uses seven horns, four trumpets, three trombones, tuba, double woodwind, cymbal, triangle, tam-tam and harp, and is fifty-two minutes long. He uses the tune 'Frère Jacques' as a round, making it sound grotesque and disturbed.

*'The term symphony – to me this means creating a world with all the technical means available.'*
Gustav Mahler

### Mahler in conversation with Freud

*'In the course of our conversation in 1910 Mahler suddenly said that he now understood why his music had always been prevented from achieving the highest rank. (Mahler's music only became fashionable and popular in the mid twentieth century.) His father, apparently a brutal person, treated his wife very badly and when Mahler was a young boy a specially painful scene caused him to rush away from the house. At that moment a hurdy-gurdy in the street was grinding out the popular Viennese air 'Ach Du Liebe Augustin'. In Mahler's opinion the conjunction of high tragedy and light amusement was from then on inextricably fixed in his mind, and the one mood inevitably brought on the other.'*

The Second Symphony, 'The Resurrection' uses a huge orchestra including voices, is in five movements, and is eighty-five minutes in length. Its first performance in 1895 used one of the biggest orchestras to date.

The Eighth Symphony is another gigantic work. Known, much to Mahler's annoyance, as the 'Symphony of a Thousand', it is in two parts, the first based on the ancient hymn 'Veni Creator Spiritus' and the second on the final scene of Goethe's *Faust*. It was the largest work he wrote, running at approximately one hour forty-five minutes. The first performance in Munich used an orchestra of 171 instrumentalists, including 22 woodwind and 24 brass and 858 singers made up of choirs from Leipzig, Munich, Vienna and 8 international soloists.

Mahler scrawled over the score of his Tenth Symphony (1906), 'Mercy, Oh God, why has thou forsaken me? – You alone know what this means. Farewell my lyre!' On the last page he writes, 'To live for you, to die for you, Almschi,' a message to Alma, his wife.

Anton Bruckner (1824–96) was a friend of Mahler. He also wrote nine symphonies and, as he was active as a cathedral musician and organist, he also wrote masses with full orchestral accompaniment. But he wrote no concertos or opera.

His symphonies are in the true Viennese tradition of four movements using 'song melodies of heavenly length'. A great admirer of Wagner, he dedicated three symphonies to him, and uses Wagner tubas in his last three symphonies. It's said that he would keep his eyes shut and just listen when attending a performance of Wagner's operas. Like Mahler, his symphonies are over an hour in length and use a large orchestra. There are several versions of each symphony because he revised his work a lot, accepting criticism from others.

His symphonies can usually be recognised at the start because he likes to begin with strings playing tremolo to give a feeling of expectancy. This is one of his trade marks.

Orchestral music has always benefited from the performance of opera. The Romantic period produced two great giants of opera, the German, Richard Wagner (1813–83) and the Italian, Guiseppe Verdi (1813–1901). Born in the same year, they both had their first success in 1842. Their different styles are endlessly compared, probably because they are diametrically opposed, yet both were successful, inhabiting totally different worlds.

Verdi wrote in the Italian style of impressive arias and grand choruses. A mark of the success of a new opera was that the delivery boys would whistle the tunes in the streets the following morning. He had a gift for writing popular melodies which would appeal to a wide audience, as they still do today – even to people who aren't usually interested in opera. Verdi went out to the world, seeking to please his public.

*'The people have always been my best friends, from the very beginning. It was a handful of carpenters who gave me my first real assurance of success.'*

Verdi

Verdi's wife and two children died in the space of two months. His new opera then failed, so he decided to give up composing. He sent his resignation to Merelli, the director of the opera house. He used to bump into Merelli in the street and one day went to the theatre (La Scala) with him. Merelli gave Verdi a libretto, which he took home, not intending to read it. The libretto fell open and he read the words, 'Go my thoughts on gilded wings.' He then read the whole thing, dismissed it and went to bed. He could not sleep. By morning he knew the verses off by heart and his new opera, *Nabucco*, was running in his head.

In Wagner's case, the world came to him, his music being much more an acquired taste. He broke down the usual conventions of opera, turning it into a continuous flow of sound without set numbers like arias and choruses. To him, opera wasn't just a showpiece for singers – it was something dramatically integrated, perfectly balanced, continuous – a life-changing experience.

Wagner's father died when he was six months old and his mother married an actor, who later introduced Richard to the theatre. He soon started writing poetry and plays, and composing music to go with them. He composed his first opera at the age of twenty. Even though he was very talented at an early age, it was a long time before he gained recognition. It wasn't until the successful performance of his opera *Rienzi* in Dresden in 1842, and his appointment as conductor of the Dresden Court Opera, that he found any security. On the strength of this, his next operas, *Flying Dutchman*, *Tannhäuser* and *Lohengrin* were performed there.

He was obliged to leave Dresden having involved himself in the political unrest there at the time. He was involved in a group, 'Young Germany', a semi-revolutionary intellectual movement. He went to stay first with Liszt in Weimar and then moved to Switzerland, where he started on an opera project which was to take him twenty years to complete (1852–74). *The Ring* is a cycle of four operas based on a mythological tale. His publishers would not accept them on the grounds that their overall length (eighteen hours) made them uncommercial. To earn a living during this time, he interrupted his work on *The Ring* to compose other operas in the three-act form. These his publishers readily accepted: *Die Meistersinger von Nürnberg* was one, *Tristan and Isolde*, another.

*Tristan and Isolde* expresses his love for Mathilde Wesen-

| **Der Ring des Nibelungen** | |
|---|---|
| **The Ring** | (1876) |
| *Das Rheingold* | |
| (The Rhinegold) | 1869 |
| *Die Walküre* | |
| (The Valkyrie) | 1870 |
| *Siegfried* | 1876 |
| *Götterdämmerung* | |
| (Twilight of the Gods) | 1876 |

donk, whose rich husband lent him money and provided him with a house on his estate. The work was one of the major achievements of his lifetime. The story is about two adulterous lovers who die for love and are then reunited in death. The whole piece is one long love duet, five hours in length, ending with Isolde's *Liebestod* (Love-death) when she dies on Tristan's body singing ecstatically of their reunion in death.

After *Tristan*, Wagner preferred to call his operas Music Dramas because the music and the drama are inseparable – the voice is treated like another instrument in the orchestra, with the poetry and music intensifying and complementing each other.

King Ludwig of Bavaria, a wildly extravagant man, invited Wagner to work as his personal adviser in Munich. Wagner happily accepted as this meant financial security, excellent resources for his operas, and an opportunity to clear his debts, for which he had almost been imprisoned in Vienna. He also knew that Ludwig, as a supporter of his music, would let him write anything he wanted. An ideal situation at last.

Wagner invited the conductor, Hans von Bülow, to be Musical Director, and promptly fell in love with his wife Cosima. Von Bülow started rehearsals of *Tristan and Isolde* on the day that Cosima's first child (by Wagner) was born. They named her Isolde. Wagner was asked to be Godfather, and the legitimacy of the child was established in order to prevent a scandal that would have lost Ludwig's financial support. Cosima and von Bülow divorced, and Wagner's wife Minna died, so eventually they married, and settled into a lifelong and devoted relationship.

It was after this that Wagner finished *The Ring* and realised his dream to build an opera house tailor-made for his music drama, in Bayreuth, where *The Ring* was first performed in

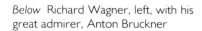

*Below* Richard Wagner, left, with his great admirer, Anton Bruckner

1876. It was here that he was finally able to take total control of his productions.

Bayreuth is a unique design in that there is a totally uninterrupted view of the stage from every seat and the orchestra pit is covered in such a way that no light from it can detract from the stage picture. The effect is similar to looking at a cinema screen. Included in the design of the theatre was elaborate stage machinery to create the many extraordinary effects required by *The Ring*: maidens swimming in the Rhine, Valkyries galloping on horseback, and huge scenic transformations.

In Bayreuth he had his ideal orchestra for *The Ring*, with over one hundred players – much larger than the usual opera orchestra. The pit was specially built to accommodate this number.

Throughout his life Wagner was a prolific writer, and set out the theory of his work which he believed to be the artwork of the future. He made up a series of terms which were central to his dramatic thinking:

*Gesamtkunstwerk*: Art should not be mere entertainment but the complete art form, made up of music, drama, poetry, dance and painting, each of equal status. In order to have complete control over each aspect of his work, he not only wrote the music, but also the libretto, and designed and choreographed the productions himself.

*Leitmotif*: a *Leitmotif* is a recurring theme which represents a character (similar to Berlioz's *idée fixe*). Wagner's operas are a web of interweaving themes of this kind. The *Leitmotif* indicates a character or object that is present on stage – or that is about to appear, or that is being thought of – like a theme tune.

In 1879 Wagner surprised Cosima on her birthday (Christmas Day) at their home near Lucerne in Switzerland with a performance of *Siegfried Idyll*, played by seventeen musicians outside her window. The piece is eighteen minutes in length. Their son, Siegfried, born before their marriage was named after the heroic character in *The Ring*.

Wagner and Verdi never met, although they planned to meet in Venice. Unfortunately, they missed each other because of a traffic jam on the canal.

*Right* Wagner, his wife Cosima and Liszt in Bayreuth

*Below right* Richard Wagner

*Below left* Extract from the original score of *Siegfried*

*Sprechgesang*: the singers are required to sing the words using the natural inflection of speech.

*Unendlichemelodie*: a melody should be uninterrupted, flowing in a continuous web without interruption.

The outer drama of Wagner's music is played out on stage while the inner psychological drama is played out in a continuous web of symphonic sound in the orchestra. They complement each other, making a completely integrated texture.

His music is extremely demanding and difficult to perform. When *Tannhäuser* was premiered the first violin part was so difficult the players just couldn't get their fingers round it.

He promoted the use of brass in the orchestra and invented a special tuba, now called the Wagner tuba, which is a cross between a horn and a trumpet. It is more versatile than other brass instruments and has a very distinctive sound and is usually played by horn players.

Wagner was well known for his anti-semitic views. It upset him that 'it is not princes who are our masters but bankers and philistines'. He tried to express his views in an essay 'Judaism in Music' in which he claimed that Jewish critics, composers and impresarios were having a negative effect on German music. His views were not uncommon for the time and his analysis of the Jews' historic role in Germany is similar to Hitler's. The difference between the views, though, is that Wagner never envisaged nor suggested Hitler's final solution – genocide. He did, however, favour the exclusion of Jews from cultural affairs.

The Judaism essay was a vicious attack on his fellow composer Meyerbeer, who was extremely hurt by it. It is said that Wagner refused to conduct the music of Mendelssohn unless

*Die Meistersinger von Nürnberg* is in some ways autobiographical in that the central character, Walter, seems to represent Wagner's personal ideals. Walter is a noble poet-musician whose song is at first derided and thought to be too strange, because it is unusual and breaks all the normal rules of song writing. But eventually he succeeds in persuading the worthy citizens of Nuremberg and the Mastersingers. He wins the girl he loves and they all live happily ever after. It has a truly optimistic, happy outcome.

When Wagner died suddenly, the grief-stricken Cosima cut off her hair and put it in the coffin because Wagner had admired it so much. She would sit by the grave for at least two hours every day and wouldn't allow anyone near it.

he was wearing gloves, because Mendelssohn was a Jew. At the end of the performance he would throw the gloves on the floor to be swept up by the cleaners.

Wagner was a complete egocentric. He called himself 'an outlaw for life. I am not made like other people. I have finer nerves. The world owes me what I need'. Society was there for his benefit to help him realise his dream, which was his only reality.

A lot of people are daunted by Wagner's music and find it heavy and difficult. Wagner was revered by Hitler and, over the years, productions of the music dramas have been heavily laden with political overtones. *The Ring*, a complex mythological story about gods, dwarves, giants and humans has been portrayed over the years as 'a manifesto for socialism, a plea for Nazi-like racism, as a forecast of the fate of the world, and as a parable about new industrial society'.

Wagner's influence on later composers is probably more all encompassing than that of any other composer, and paved the way for the future with its chromatic harmonies, and profoundly disturbing emotions which never rest.

Perhaps Mahler's comment was a premonition of what lay ahead: 'Imagine the universe begins to vibrate and resound. These are no longer human voices, but planets and suns revolving.'

One of Wagner's contemporaries, Rossini, said: 'This is what Wagner's music sounds like.' Opening the piano and sitting himself heavily on the keys, he exclaimed, 'There, that's the music of the future.' Ironically, as it turned out, there was more truth than Rossini could have foretold in his insult.

# The Brass

Brass instruments were originally outdoor instruments used for hunting, military functions, public and religious occasions. The early instruments were very simple and could only be used within the limitations of their quite restricted range. Like the woodwind, the sound is created by blowing down a mouthpiece into varying lengths of tubing. A hollow metal tube produces a sequence of notes (a 'harmonic series') depending on how it is blown.

The brass section in a modern orchestra usually consists of four horns, two or three trumpets, three trombones (two tenor and one bass) and a tuba. Similar to the woodwind, the instruments (except for the horn) come in families of different sizes, according to tuning.

Around 1815 a special system of valves was invented which enabled brass instruments to play more notes and be more accurate. This liberated the instruments and gave them a whole new status in the orchestra, establishing them as a section in their own right. Romantic composers used them to carry important tunes not just to add strength to a climax in the music.

The inventor of the valve is said to be Heinrich Stolzel, a horn player, who made use of the invention in Berlin and got involved with a bandsman Friedrich Bluhmel, who later claimed to have invented it. The design was patented in Prussia in 1818 and by 1830 they were in use all over Europe. The valve enabled the player to change the length of the tube at a single touch and therefore be more versatile on the instrument.

The earliest horn was an animal horn but the instrument

Sounds from a brass instrument are created by blowing a raspberry into the mouthpiece in a controlled way. Tensing the lips creates high notes, slackening them, low notes. It seems simple, but to make a good sound on a brass instrument takes a great deal of skill and energy.

we know today is the descendant of the simple French hunting horn (hence its name 'French horn') which was just a piece of coiled tube with a bell at the end. Until the valve was invented, players of the natural horn were restricted to the number of notes they could play on one length of tubing. The first orchestral music written for horn (Lully is credited as being the first to introduce the horn into the orchestra in 1664) was simple and followed the basic patterns of notes the instrument could achieve naturally. It was then discovered that by putting the hand inside the bell in different positions, extra notes could be created, and extensions of different sizes (crooks) could be added to change the length of the tube and therefore achieve extra notes. There are nine different sizes of crook.

The modern valve horn is an expressive and colourful instrument. It combines all the different crooks in one instrument, making twelve feet of tubing altogether. Once the valve was invented the use of the natural horn declined because it could not play the complicated music required of the instrument – in pieces by Wagner, for instance.

Unlike the other brass instruments, there is only one type of horn. It has three characteristic sounds: deep and solid in its low register; bright and heroic in its middle register; brilliant and loud in its top register.

From the invention of the valve onwards, music for horn became much more demanding. It is the only left-handed instrument of the orchestra, and it plays backwards, in that the bell faces backwards. Sometimes you can play 'quivre' which means you hold the bell up to play very loudly. Some of the best music for the horn is written in orchestral music.

Trumpets come in many different sizes. Like the clarinet, they are a transposing instrument – you pick your trumpet according to the key of music to be played. Their history goes

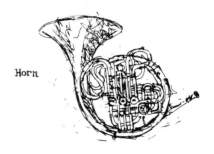

Horn

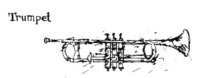

Trumpet

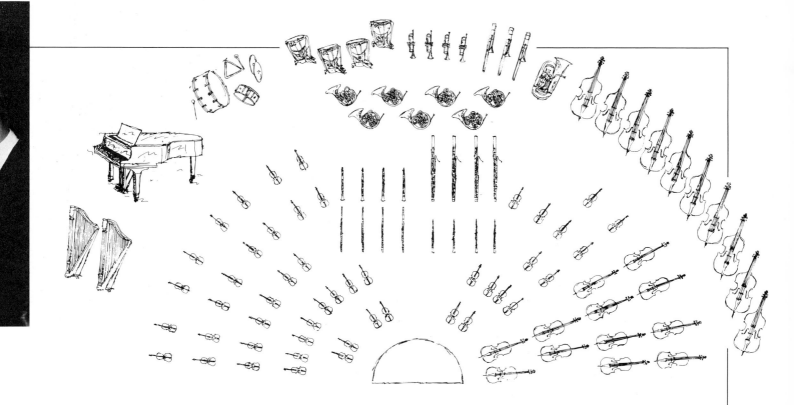

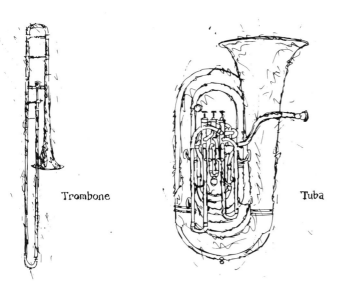

The orchestra layout for a Romantic work. The layout will vary today as it would have done during the Romantic period; the above plan is based on the one Sir Georg Solti would use with the Chicago Symphony Orchestra

Trombone

Tuba

It is very tiring to play a brass instrument for long stretches without a break. For this reason it is common to have an extra player, especially in horn and trumpet sections, known as the 'bumper'. This player reinforces the section and enables other players to take a rest.

back a long way – two straight trumpets were found in the tomb of Tutankhamen. Descended from the animal bone also, the early trumpets were valveless and resembled a bugle. In the Baroque era there was a fashion for virtuoso trumpet playing on an instrument called a clarino (small trumpet). The demands made on the trumpet at this time rival those made on the violin. Its piercing, brilliant sound easily stands out against other orchestral instruments (as in 'The Trumpet Shall Sound', in Handel's *Messiah*). It then went into decline in the eighteenth century because this sound was no longer in fashion, only to be revived with the invention of the valve in the mid-nineteenth century. For a while, the trumpet players used crooks, like the horn, to extend the range of the instrument. Now the trumpet has piston valves, which are slightly different from the horn valves, but serve the same purpose. Otherwise the basic instrument has changed little over the years.

The curled tubing of the early trumpets was about eight feet long. The tubing of the modern instrument is much shorter, only about four feet long, and the instruments are made in different sizes and tunings: B flat, C, D, E, piccolo trumpet and cornets. The B flat and C trumpets are the most regular orchestral trumpets, but a trumpet player could carry anything up to four instruments with him. It is for the player to decide which instrument to use – and he may use several different ones to perform one piece of music.

Playing the small clarino trumpet in Bach's music is wonderful because of the 'brilliance' of the sound. Playing Berlioz, Wagner and Strauss is much more fun than playing Mozart because there is more solo music to play.

There are several different types of 'mute' which can be used to dampen the sound of the trumpet. They come in different sizes: wow-wow, cup, plunger and bucket, and fit in the bell of the instrument.

There are usually three trombones in the modern symphony orchestra – two tenor trombones and one bass trombone. The earliest trombones were the bass trombones, tuned in F. Now the tenor trombone, tuned in B flat, is also used.

In the fourteenth century a trumpet with a slide was called 'trombone' (Italian for 'large trumpet'). The French then made them, calling them a *saqueboute* (pull-push). The English took them over as sackbuts, which were made in a variety of sizes.

The instrument doesn't have valves and hasn't changed much over the years. It uses a slide to create the notes, which requires the player's judgement to find the correct position. It's similar to a violin in that there is nothing to tell you where to put your fingers to create the notes. You have to 'feel' them.

In the sixteenth century players used four instruments, soprano, alto, tenor and bass, to correspond to the human voice. They tended to be used a lot in church music because of their dark, sombre sound. (Beethoven was the first to use it as a regular member of the orchestra, in his Fifth Symphony.)

Three trombones playing together can sound very loud and awe-inspiring. A full blast from them can really deafen the musicians sitting in front. But they are also able to play very quietly and are good at sliding from note to note (glissando).

The tuba is easy to recognise by its huge size at the back of the orchestra, and it forms the bass of the brass section. Over the years attempts had been made to create a truly bass brass instrument. The ophicleide and various other brass instruments had tried to fulfil this role, but were unsuccessful. The orchestral bass tuba was invented by Johann Gottfried Moritz in 1829 and was first used by Berlioz, instead of the ophicleide, in the Symphonie fantastique in 1830. Wagner was

There are only a handful of concertos for trombone, but they have many beautiful solos in orchestral music.

Wagner enjoyed using brass in his opera orchestra, giving them an important dramatic role. He invented a special tuba, known as the Wagner tuba, which is usually played by a horn player because of the shape of the mouthpiece.

fascinated by the tuba and helped develop a whole family of them. There are now about five or six different instruments of varying ranges and lengths, from nine to sixteen feet. The big bass tuba emerged in 1845, but there are other lighter, more elegant instruments, especially the Wagner tuba, whose range fits between the horn and the trumpet and is noticeable in the orchestra because of its gracefully angled bell.

To look at a bass tuba is a bit like being in the basement looking at the central heating system. It dismantles in a similar way to a French horn. There are various different sizes of tuba to suit the range of the music.

The instrument speaks a bit sluggishly at the bottom of its range, getting more agile when it gets higher. As it takes a great deal of breath to blow, tuba players often use the technique of rotary breathing, which means breathing in and blowing out at the same time, achieved by holding the breath in the mouth. Like the other brass instruments, it can be muted. Various concertos have been written for the tuba by composers like Vaughan Williams, Derek Bourgeois and others. And it has some excellent solos in orchestral music, for example, at the end of the Prelude to *Die Meistersinger* where the bass tuba carries the main theme. But its comic nature was probably immortalised by George Kleinsinger's music for Paul Tripp's children's story *Tubby the Tuba* (1944) where the hero is, of course, the tuba, narrated by Danny Kaye.

# The Twentieth Century

All periods of music history so far seem to have emphasised one particular aspect of music: first the voice (the Renaissance); then the liberation of instruments (the Baroque); the consolidation of different forms of music and the shape of the orchestra (the Classical); stretching the limits of these forms through passionate self-expression (the Romantics); and now the twentieth century, in which music apparently bursts at the seams with the continuing experimentation with new sounds.

From 1900 onwards, composers made a series of dramatic and courageous leaps. Works like Richard Strauss's operas *Salomé* (1905) and *Elektra* (1909), Schoenberg's opera, *Erwartung* (1909), and Stravinsky's *The Rite of Spring* (1913) were strikingly provocative and shocked audiences, shaking the very foundations on which music up to that time had been built. One could say that these changes were precipitated by the chromatic harmonies of Wagner – it was impossible to avoid his influence. A lot of orchestral music at the beginning of the century sounded as if it was heading for a nervous breakdown, and in a sense it was – heading for the breakdown of tonality, out of which the music of the future would emerge.

For the sake of convenience, the twentieth century can be divided into three parts. The first is the period up to the First World War (1914), when the Romantic composers made their final utterances and various composers, like Stravinsky and Schoenberg, were taking their first steps into the future. The second is the period between the two World Wars, when some of the most far-reaching changes took place. The third part is from 1945 onwards, when the new ideas were picked up again after the Second World War, which had delayed some composers' progress because, in countries invaded by Germany, only music recognised by the Third Reich was permitted to be performed. Although composers affected by this continued to write and (illegally) perform their music, many of the manuscripts were lost as a result of the war.

The search for new sounds meant a search for new instruments to create them. Composers began to use unusual objects as musical instruments – sandpaper and teacups (Britten's *Noye's Fludde*); motor horns (Gershwin's *An American in Paris*); a police whistle (Ibert); recorded nightingale (Resphigi); iron chains (Schoenberg's *Gurrelieder*); short-wave radio (Stock-

*'Music is no different from opium. Music affects the human mind in a way that makes people think of nothing but music and sensual matters – music is treason to the country, a treason to our youth, and should be cut out and replaced with something instructive.'*
The Ayatollah Khomeini
1979

hausen); recorded heartbeat (Tippett's Fourth Symphony); wind machine (Vaughan Williams' *Sinfonia Antartica*). Eventually, anything that made a sound, from typewriters to spoons, could qualify as a musical instrument – and even the background noises of everyday life have been considered music by John Cage.

At the beginning of the twentieth century, rhythms became harsher and more violent. Percussion instruments were used increasingly to emphasise rhythm, with many new instruments arriving from the Far East and Latin America. The orchestra, ever bigger and more powerful, included a large percussion section, harps and the piano on a regular basis, and now opened its doors to many new instruments. The percussion could give new colour to the sound, with the use of keyboard instruments such as xylophones, glockenspiels, marimbas and vibraphones.

Although the growth of classical music is usually thought of only in relation to the Western World, centred on Europe, by the 1900s America and Australia were also producing influential composers and orchestras. Western music was known in the Far East, but in the twentieth century, Eastern composers have also taken to writing in Western styles. Some of the most notable are the Japanese Toshi Ichiyanagi, Toshiro Mayuzumi, Fukushima and Toro Takemitsu, and the Matsudairas; the Korean Isang Yun and the Chinese Chou Wen Chung.

The dramatic improvements in communication have made the musical world truly international: radio, the gramophone, air travel, film, the telephone, the motor car, and recorded sound have all served to open up the world. The gramophone (invented in 1887), radio and later television, brought the symphony orchestra into the home for the first time and

*If ever I cross the Atlantic again, I want a most exclusive cabin in a very fast boat for me and my Missus to keep undesirable people away. But what I really want is to keep off the sea altogether. I'm fed up with the ship, the passengers and the noise. I am expecting great things at Yale – nice men, a quiet room, one or two walks. Also my lecture is the least bad I have ever written. When I get home I want to live a humdrum monotonous existence with lots of routine work, the occasional conducting job and three-day walks.*

Holst, letter to his wife from on board HMS *Scythis*, 1929

made music available to a wide audience. The first recorded symphony was Beethoven's Fifth in 1909, played by the Berlin Philharmonic.

Once again, as in all periods of classical music, there is a time when styles overlap, some rocketing us into the future and others consolidating the past. In the early 1900s, we find two composers in Paris, one a Russian, the other a Frenchman. Stravinsky blasts the audience out of their seats with the violent, strident rhythms of his ballet, *The Rite of Spring*; Debussy, who is gently cultivating his own unique style of Impressionism in the wake of the Wagner epidemic, seduces them with his flowing, contemplative symphonic masterpieces.

Igor Stravinsky (1882–1971) grew up in a musical family – his father was an opera singer who took him to opera and ballet when he was a child. His parents were quite well off, and sent him to university to study law, but, like Handel, he gave up law after his father died. His big breakthrough came when the impresario, Sergei Diaghilev, heard his music and asked him to write a work for the Ballets Russes, who were famous for their Paris seasons. He wrote *The Firebird*, which was a huge success – so he immediately wrote another, *Petrushka*, which was equally successful. *The Rite of Spring*, his third ballet, also written for Diaghilev, launched his international career.

Diaghilev first heard *The Rite of Spring* when Stravinsky played it to him on the piano in the Grand Hotel in Venice. Playing an orchestral work on the piano was the usual way of introducing a new composition to an impresario or promoter, in the hope of getting a commitment to perform it. Stravinsky later said that Diaghilev didn't really understand the music, but could see that it had commercial potential.

When asked to declare his profession when passing through customs, Stravinsky described himself on one occasion as an 'Inventor'.

Subtitled 'Pictures of Pagan Russia', the music describes an ancient fertility rite, the sacrifice of a virgin to placate the powers of earth. Short phrases, hedonistic rhythms, and percussive effects all express the primitive elements of the story. It is written for a large orchestra of over one hundred players. No one anywhere had seen or heard anything like it before and time hasn't softened its impact.

*'My music is best understood by children and animals.'*
Igor Stravinsky

On the opening night at the Théâtre des Champs Elysées on 29 May 1913, the audience started shouting and screaming seconds after curtain up. Nijinsky, the choreographer, had to stand on a chair in the wings shouting numbers at the dancers, who could no longer hear the music because of the noise in the auditorium. The audience were upset not only by the music, but by the way the dancers hurled themselves around

### The Rite of Spring

Stravinsky's own account of the opening performance of *The Rite of Spring*:

I was sitting in the fourth or fifth row on the right and the image of Monteux's [the conductor] back is more vivid in my mind today than the picture of the stage. He stood there apparently impervious and as nerveless as a crocodile. It is still almost incredible to me that he brought the orchestra through to the end. I left my seat when the heavy noises began and went backstage behind Nijinsky in the right wing. He was standing on a chair just out of view of the audience, shouting numbers at the dancers. I wondered what on earth these numbers had to to with the music. From what I heard, the musical performance was not bad – they had sixteen full rehearsals so the orchestra was quite secure. After the performance we were excited, angry, disgusted and . . . happy. I went with Diaghilev and Nijinsky to a restaurant. Diaghilev's only comment was: 'Exactly what I wanted.' He certainly looked contented. Perhaps he had already thought about the possibility of such a scandal when I played it to him months before, in Venice.

Pierre Monteux recalls the first performance:

You may think it's strange, but I have never seen the ballet. The night of the premiere I kept my eyes on the score, playing the exact tempo Igor had given me and which, I must say, I have never forgotten. As you know, the public reacted in a scandalous manner. The gendarmes arrived at last. On hearing the near riot behind me I decided to keep the orchestra together at any cost in case of a lull in the hubbub. I did, and we played it to the end exactly as we had rehearsed it. We played it in London a few times to very polite audiences. Then, as the saying goes, the work was 'shelved'.

The impresario Sergei Diaghilev (1872–1929)

the stage. The police arrived, but the performance continued to the end. Critics said at the time, 'It has no relation to music,' but sixteen years later, the piece was hailed as 'one of the most significant landmarks in the artistic life of the period'. After the opening night there were five more performances and each time the audience reacted in the same way. Later, the conductor Pierre Monteux persuaded Stravinsky to let him conduct it in a theatre as a concert piece. This performance was sold out, with everyone from Parisian musical circles in attendance. Monteux's mother sat in a box with the French composer Camille Saint-Saëns, who just repeated over and over again, 'Mais il est fou, il est fou!' ('He's crazy, he's crazy.') Monteux reports that the musicians performing it at this concert who had also played it for the premiere, felt differently about it now. They told him the music had already aged.

Shortly after *The Rite of Spring* was first performed, Stravinsky fell seriously ill with typhoid and eventually went to live in Switzerland. He never returned to Russia after the Revolution and moved to America in 1939 when the Second World War broke out.

He was always experimenting with new styles. He had started off writing in the Russian style, having been taught by Rimsky-Korsakov at the Academy of Music in St Petersburg. From about 1917 he developed a neo-Classical style, taking up forms used in the Classical era and using them with modern harmonies, producing *The Soldier's Tale* (for a group of instrumentalists), *Oedipus Rex* (an opera/oratorio) and *The Symphony of Psalms* (for chorus and orchestra). America gave him access to other media such as films and music for stage plays.

In his first years in Hollywood, Stravinsky badly needed money. His early works, registered in Tsarist Russia, were

*'Stravinsky's working table was an incredible sight. It looked like an architect's drawing board – everything laid out neatly, pencils sharpened in three colours. He said to me, "I can only compose if my desk is absolutely clear, because when my desk is clear, then my mind is clear also."'*

Sir Georg Solti

*'Pay no attention to critics. Remember, no statue has ever been put up in honour of a critic.'*

Jean Sibelius, attr.

*'I answered the phone in Hollywood one day and a voice said, "This is Stravinsky." I nearly dropped dead. It was like God ringing me up.'*

Sir Georg Solti

Billy Rose commissioned music from Stravinsky for a New York revue, staged in 1945. On the opening night, he cabled the composer:

YOUR MUSIC GREAT SUCCESS STOP COULD BE SENSATIONAL SUCCESS IF YOU WOULD AUTHORISE ROBERT BENNETT RETOUCH ORCHESTRATION STOP BENNETT ORCHESTRATES EVEN THE WORKS OF COLE PORTER STOP

Stravinsky replied:

SATISFIED WITH GREAT SUCCESS.

Claude Debussy and, seated, Igor Stravinsky

Original manuscripts are now sold for huge sums. Sotheby's in London report that nine Mozart symphonies went for £2,350,000 in 1987; a Schubert overture for £150,000 in 1986; a Beethoven sonata for £480,000; and a Bach cantata for £390,000 in 1989. In November 1982, Stravinsky's *Rite of Spring* was sold for £300,000.

not protected by copyright and earned him no income. The film producer Louis B. Mayer offered him a job: 'I hear you are the greatest composer in the world,' he said. 'Well, this is the greatest movie studio in the world!' Mayer asked him how much he would charge for a score forty-five minutes long. Stravinsky said $25,000. Mayer remarked that this was more money than they normally paid, but since he was the greatest composer in the world, he would be paid it. When Stravinsky said the score would take about one year to write, Mayer showed him the door. When asked why he charged such large fees, Stravinsky said, 'I do it on behalf of my brother composers, Mozart and Schubert, who died in poverty.'

Stravinsky said the only musician who really understood

*The Rite of Spring* at the time was Maurice Ravel (1875–1937). Ravel stayed with Stravinsky in Clarens during March and April 1913, just before *The Rite of Spring* was produced. Their friendship is revealed in the many letters they wrote to each other. In December 1913, when Stravinsky was very ill with typhoid, Ravel wrote:

> Vieux – it's a long time since I've had any sensational news about your health. Three weeks ago I heard about your sudden death, but was not stricken by it as the same morning we received a postcard from you. I will be in London in three days and hope to hear talk about *Le Sacre* [*The Rite of Spring*]. My compliments to Mme Stravinsky, kiss the children and believe in the affection of your devoted – Maurice Ravel.

A curious, lonely character, Ravel devoted his life to his mother. A recluse when composing, he also loved Paris night-life. Stravinsky said of him, 'He was dry and reserved and sometimes little darts were hidden in his remarks, but he was always a good friend to me. He drove a truck in the war and I admired him for it. He could have had an easier time. He looked rather pathetic in his uniform; so small.'

Ravel never married and said that artists 'are rarely normal, and our lives are even less so'. At the premiere of *Bolero*, one of his most famous works, a woman in the audience cried out 'He's mad!' and Ravel nodded in agreement.

Ravel is usually thought of as an Impressionist, like Debussy, although his orchestral sound was unmistakeably his own. He once said he wanted to write a treatise on orchestration illustrated with examples of failures from his own works. But in fact, he was a virtuoso orchestrator, a master of intricate and dazzling instrumentation. He treats the orchestra

*'When I met Stravinsky, I asked him why he had reorchestrated* The Rite of Spring *and made it more simple. He replied that it was so he could conduct it – the original was too difficult. Later friends told me that the real reason was that he got no royalties from the Russian edition, so he did a new edition for Boosey & Hawkes so he could get some money.'*

Sir Georg Solti

Although *Bolero* brought Ravel widespread fame, he never became rich from his music – it seems he probably had private means. He liked to dress fashionably, and once spent a fortune on a blue tailcoat to wear to a soirée in Paris. He was mortified to overhear someone saying, 'Who is that little fellow who didn't bother to dress?'

Maurice Ravel

like a magical machine, fitting the instruments together in a way which made Stravinsky call him a 'Swiss watchmaker'. Berlioz said that instrumentation in music is the exact equivalent of colour in painting. Ravel is living proof of this.

Like Stravinsky, Ravel wrote ballets for Diaghilev, *Daphne and Chloé* being the best known. In 1914 he started writing a symphonic poem called *Wien*, based on the Viennese waltz. It was an appropriate subject at the time, because there was a general feeling of anger that the aristocrats were still dancing in Vienna and ignoring the war. He was unable to complete the piece because he had to start military service. After the war, in 1919, he moved back to live in the country again and tried to start work on a new ballet for Diaghilev. He was finding it difficult to work as he was still upset over the recent death of his mother, so he decided to re-work *Wien*, giving it the new title, *La Valse*, and writing two versions of it for piano solo and two pianos. He then orchestrated it in three months. The orchestral version is thirteen minutes long; its main theme is played at first by muted violins with the bow 'over the fingerboard', which makes them sound ghostly. Eventually, this tune is taken up exuberantly by the full orchestra and distorted in a very disturbing way. Scored for a large orchestra, the piece requires a full string section, triple or quadruple woodwind, full brass, two harps and a percussion section including castanets, gong, glockenspiel and antique cymbals. He invited Diaghilev and Stravinsky, his trusted friends, to a private hearing, playing it to them on the piano. Diaghilev thought it a masterpiece, but not a ballet, and refused to stage it. Stravinsky, apparently, said nothing. Ravel took the score and walked out. It was the end of his friendship with Diaghilev, whom he challenged to a duel when they met again in 1925 in Monte Carlo.

The first performance was given in a concert hall on 12 December 1920 and since then *La Valse* has been played all over the world successfully as a concert piece. Ravel described, on the front of the score, the stage picture he imagined but which was never designed:

> Through rifts in the eddying clouds are glimpsed a waltzing couple. Gradually clouds disperse and an immense hall is seen, thronged with a whirling crowd. The full light of the chandeliers bursts out. An Imperial Court about 1855.

He said when he was writing this piece that he felt a 'fantastic and fatal whirling'. The reviews praised the 'dazzling orchestration', but did not like the 'truculence and frenzy of the conclusion'.

*'I think Ravel knew when he went into hospital for the last operation that he would go to sleep for the last time. He said to me, "They can do what they want with my cranium as long as the ether works." It didn't work and the poor man felt the incision. My last view of him was in the funeral home. The top part of his skull was still bandaged. The last years of his life were cruel because he was losing his memory and his coordinating powers and, of course, was quite aware of it.'*

Igor Stravinsky

Diaghilev died laughing, and singing *La Bohème*, his favourite music.

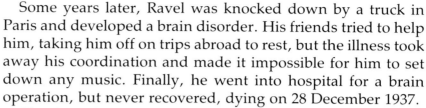

*'There is no sign of music changing at all. A dissonant chord would cause a revolution.'*

Debussy, letter to
Emile Barron, 1887

Some years later, Ravel was knocked down by a truck in Paris and developed a brain disorder. His friends tried to help him, taking him off on trips abroad to rest, but the illness took away his coordination and made it impossible for him to set down any music. Finally, he went into hospital for a brain operation, but never recovered, dying on 28 December 1937.

Claude Debussy (1862–1918) also wrote a ballet for Diaghilev: *Jeux*, which opened in the same year as *The Rite of Spring*, but without the same impact. He is usually thought of as the leading Impressionist, a term he hated, which was taken from a group of French writers (Mallarmé, for example) and painters (Monet, Renoir and Manet, among others). His music gives the 'impression' of a picture or event by using very subtle, undefined sounds.

He became interested in the music of Bali and Java after hearing the Gamelan orchestra at the Paris World Exposition in 1889. A lot of artists in Paris at this time were fascinated by the Orient and also Ancient Greece. Debussy, too, rediscovered ancient styles of music and the technique of the whole-tone scale, which is like playing only the black notes on the piano.

All his music for the orchestra is descriptive, the first work being *Prelude à l'Après Midi d'un Faune* (1894), based on a poem by Mallarmé, and perhaps his most famous being the three Symphonic Sketches: *La Mer* (1905). It is said that he composed the last movement of *La Mer* over-

133

looking the sea in the south of England, in the Grand Hotel in Eastbourne. Debussy uses a large orchestra, but does not use its size solely to create volume. Like Ravel, his interest was colour. The strings are often muted, and he uses the contemplative sounds of flute, oboe and cor anglais for many solos, and a large percussion section including xylophone, tam-tam, celeste, glockenspiel and cymbals.

He wrote an opera in 1902, *Pelléas and Mélisande*, which is a love story. When the couple finally declare their love for each other, it is exquisitely sung on one note – the antithesis of the expression of love-death in Wagner's *Tristan and Isolde*.

There were other composers in France who reacted against both Romanticism and Impressionism, trying to find a smaller, more popular style. They modelled themselves on Erik Satie, whose music is on a small scale, with a very touching and nostalgic quality, and called themselves 'Les Six': Arthur Honegger, Darius Milhaud, Francis Poulenc, Auric, Tailleferre and Durey.

Composers at this time wanted to reveal the special qualities of their homeland by using folk songs and other national characteristics as an integral part of their music. In some countries, nationalism was expressed by using the traditional symphonic style and in others, by breaking into more innovative forms.

One of the earliest nationalist composers was Anton Dvořàk (1841–1904). He uses Czech folk-dance rhythms in his music, especially in his orchestral work, the Slavonic Dances. After his Third Symphony won a prize in 1873, Brahms became very interested in his music and helped and encouraged him. Only five of Dvořàk's nine symphonies were published in his lifetime, the most well known being 'From the New World' (1893). His Cello Concerto (1895) is one of the sublime master-

*Satie thought it might be amusing to compose music not to be listened to – 'musique d'ameublement', or wallpaper music. Once, his music started and people began to return to their seats. He pleaded with them, 'Carry on talking! Walk about! Don't listen!' But no one paid any attention to him.*

Darius Milhaud,
*Notes About Music*

pieces in the repertoire. Unfortunately, though, he was very poor all his life because he sold his compositions for a pittance, and was forced to live in circumstances which a friend of his described as being 'like a scene from *La Bohème.'*

Jean Sibelius (1865–1957), working in Finland, was one of the most admired living symphonists between the two World Wars, composing seven symphonies by 1924, and he remains Finland's best-known composer. Like Carl Nielsen, his Danish contemporary, Sibelius felt a strong national commitment, possibly as his country was under Russian rule until 1917, which he expressed in his most famous work, *Finlandia* (1899). His symphonies mostly start in one key and finish in another (like Mahler), and are of average length (30-40 minutes), but they vary in their number of movements. Sibelius did not extend the orchestral resources or add voices, but his symphonies vividly express the vast open spaces of his homeland.

In Russia, a group of musicians calling themselves 'The Five', Borodin, Rimsky-Korsakov, Mussorgsky, Cui and Balakirev, based their music on stories from Russian history. They were unusual in that they had no formal musical training: Borodin, for instance, was a chemist, Rimsky-Korsakov an ex-naval officer, and Mussorgsky a civil servant, yet they were highly skilled orchestrators. Rimsky-Korsakov, probably the most brilliant of them all, wrote a book, *The Principles of Orchestration*, in 1913. The pianist, Sergey Rachmaninov, joined them for a while, but then fled Russia for the USA before the Revolution in 1917 and never returned.

Béla Bartók (1881–1945) grew up in Hungary and worked as a teacher in Budapest until 1934. He was a devoted nationalist, collecting literally thousands of Hungarian and other folk tunes and using them in his music. He told his mother when

*'They talk of nothing but money and jobs. Give me businessmen anytime – they really are interested in music and art.'*

Jean Sibelius on musicians

*Below* Sergey Rachmaninov

135

Otto Klemperer, the conductor was a pupil of Bartók. He said of him:

'He was a wonderful pianist. The beauty, energy and lightness of his tone were unforgettable.'

he was young that his one objective in life was to work for 'the good of Hungary and the Hungarian nation'.

Bartók uses an unusual arrangement for the orchestra in his Music for Strings, Percussion and Celeste (1936), dividing the strings into two small chamber groups placed either side of a a piano, harp, celeste, and percussion section. He treats the instruments in a percussive, highly rhythmic way, his own instrument, the piano, being a central feature.

Bartók was deeply upset by the brutality of war and was one of the first to speak out against anti-semitism, forbidding his music to be played in Germany in the 1930s. He made his American debut as a pianist in 1927, finally returning there to live in 1940, to escape the Nazis. His research grant from Columbia University enabled him to stay in New York, but he was never well off. Bartók became very ill with leukemia and was being treated in hospital, although he had not been

The Concerto for Orchestra is in four movements and is thirty-seven minutes long. Bartók called it a concerto rather than a symphony because each section of the orchestra has an important solo part. It is scored for three flutes, three oboes, three clarinets and three bassoons; four horns, three trumpets, three trombones and tuba; kettledrums, snare drums, bass drum, cymbals, triangle, tam-tam, two harps and strings.

told the true nature of his illness. A friend secured a commission in order to bring him some income, arriving at the hospital with the cheque in his pocket. But Bartók's high principles would not allow him to accept the full fee until the music was written. It was the Concerto for Orchestra (1944), which was the only work to bring him success in his lifetime. Unfortunately, though, this came too late to help him, for he died a year later.

In England, Edward Elgar (1857–1934) was the first English-born composer to have a firm place in the international repertory of symphony, concerto and overture. His choral work, *The Dream of Gerontius* (1900) and the *Enigma Variations* (1899) put him on the map. His characteristic style of orchestration is best heard in his two symphonies (1908, 1911), each in four movements, in the *Enigma Variations*, in his concertos – one for violin and one for cello – and in his overtures. His orchestration is exuberant and his music has great patriotic fervour, reflecting the spirit of England after the First World War. In his famous overture about London, the *Cockaigne*, he uses the organ, imitates marching bands, small bells and a triangle represent the jingle of a horse's harness, and he uses tunes to represent the characters of London.

Ralph Vaughan Williams (1872–1958) was also a great symphonist, and also collected and arranged English folk songs. Like Bartók, he amassed a vast number of long-forgotten pieces, re-orchestrated them and used them as themes in his compositions.

Gustav Holst (1874–1934) – of Swedish parentage but born in Cheltenham – wrote a series of symphonic sketches in the style of a symphonic poem, *The Planets* (1920) which in England was thought to be outrageously forward thinking at the time and rocketed him to fame!

Edward Elgar

*I've learnt what Classical means. It means something that sings and dances through sheer joy of existence.*

Holst to
Vaughan Williams

Ralph Vaughan Williams

Gustav Holst and Ralph Vaughan Williams were great friends. They wrote to each other regularly from wherever they were working and gave each other much support and encouragement. They also discussed philosophical issues about composing:

*I hope you bear in mind that the rot I write is a collection of stray thoughts . . . Sometimes when things turn out an awful failure it may teach us more than a thundering success. It does not follow that it WILL but it MAY. As I told you before, Richard [Strauss] seems to me to be the most 'Beethovenish' composer since Beethoven. Perhaps I am wrong but I hope you will agree that, whatever his faults, he is a real life composer. As far as I can make out, his training seems to have been:*
*1 Bach, Mozart, Beethoven*
*2 Schumann, Brahms*
*3 Wagner*

*Mine has been:*
*1 Mendelssohn*
*2 Grieg*
*3 Wagner*

*This alone speaks volumes. I believe, as you once said, that every composer is the result of those who have gone before him. So, you and I must begin to feel this about ourselves.*

Letter from Holst to
Vaughan Williams, Dresden 1903

*I really cannot feel concerned about your fears that all your invention has gone. I am sorry, but it is impossible. You got into the same state of mind just before you wrote the* Heroic Elegy, *so that I look upon it as a good sign and quite expect to hear that you have struck oil when you write again.*

Letter from Holst to Vaughan Williams,
Berlin 1903

Sir William Walton (1902–83) was at first thought mildly shocking because he produced *Façade*, a sequence of eighteen poems by Edith Sitwell in which he uses jazz rhythms, and shows his strong sense of humour. His coronation march, *Crown Imperial* (1937), is in Elgar's style of grand gesture. His First Symphony (1935), of two, is in four movements and forty-five minutes long and is written in the traditional symphonic style. Other important orchestral works by him are the overture, *Portsmouth Point*; the Viola Concerto, Violin Concerto, Cello Concerto and the Cantata for Choir and Orchestra, *Belshazzar's Feast* (1931). He also wrote film music, with scores for films such as *Henry V*, which has been played as a concert piece ever since.

Benjamin Britten (1913–76) was the first English composer since Purcell to write outstanding operas – *Peter Grimes*, *Albert Herring*, *The Rape of Lucretia* and the *Turn of the Screw*, for example – and to be internationally acknowledged for it. The orchestral work which launched him as a composer was *Variations on a Theme of Frank Bridge* in 1937, written for a full-sized orchestra as a commission for the Salzburg Festival. The *War Requiem* of 1962 places the war poems of Wilfred Owen in the liturgical framework of the requiem. In 1946 he wrote *The Young Person's Guide to the Orchestra*, which is a set of variations and fugue based on a tune by Purcell. First the main theme is stated by the full orchestra, then each instrument takes it up in turn as a way of introducing themselves. His lifelong partnership with the singer Sir Peter Pears inspired a great deal of music, including his Serenade for Tenor, Horn and Strings. He was also friends with the poet W.H. Auden, having met him when they worked together in the Post Office film unit in the 1930s.

Sir Michael Tippett, born in 1905, writes all forms of orches-

William Walton

Tippett and Britten first met during the Second World War when they were both conscientious objectors. Tippett had been sent to prison for breaking the law applying to conscientious objectors and Britten and Sir Peter Pears went to give a concert at Wormwood Scrubs prison where he was being detained. The three had wanted to play a concert together, so Tippett made an excuse that he had to turn the pages, so he could be up on the platform with them.

Above right Michael Tippett, left, and Benjamin Britten

Above Benjamin Britten

tral music; concertos, symphonies and opera. He has composed a triple concerto for the combination of violin, viola and cello (1979), the only example of a concerto for this combination of instruments. Tippett once asked himself, 'Has the reality of my imagination any lasting relation to the reality of those events which immediately affect the lives of men?' and he has given a lot of time to social problems and helping other people. He openly acknowledges his debt to Beethoven and also uses American traditional music, jazz, spirituals and blues, as shown in his pacifist oratorio, *A Child of our Time*, which, first performed in 1944, established him as a major composer.

His Fourth Symphony was first performed in America by

the Chicago Symphony Orchestra in 1977. Of his four symphonies, it is the only one in one movement. The orchestra includes six horns and a large percussion section. At the beginning, breathing is heard, created either by a wind machine or percussionists breathing heavily. In it, he uses themes from Elizabethan England.

Dmitri Shostakovich (1906–75) was one of the most important composers of the century, and wrote fifteen symphonies. Unlike his contemporary, Sergei Prokofiev (1891–1953), he grew up in Russia as she was recovering from the Revolution and throughout his life had problems with the authorities, who banned his music on more than one occasion. Shostakovich's First Symphony – in four movements, and about thirty minutes in length – was performed in 1926, when he was twenty years old. The orchestration was so original that the conductor remarked at the end of the performance that he felt he had turned over 'a new page in the history of symphonic music'. His music is extremely powerful, and seems to express the confusion and fear felt in Russia at that time. He said about his music, 'By studying my works you will find the whole truth about me as a man and an artist.'

America also emerged as a leading force in orchestral music. Unlike Europe, its classical music heritage was only a hundred years old at the turn of the century, having taken hold with the formation of the Handel and Haydn Society in Boston in 1815. Since then, America has made many significant contributions to classical music and the advancement of the orchestra, providing a new home for many expatriate composers fleeing the political troubles in Europe and Russia. Composers

For several years, Shostakovich's music was banned by the Soviet authorities. His Fifth Symphony had to be approved by the Party Aktiv before it could be performed. Galina Vishnevskaya reports in her book, 'A few dozen nincompoops got together to judge a genius. The symphony was performed and resounded throughout the world. We hear desecrated Russia, violated by her own sons, wailing and writhing in agony.' In February 1948, Shostakovich was denounced as a 'formalist' and banned from teaching in the Moscow and Leningrad Conservatoires. Stalin died in 1953 and Shostakovich wrote his Tenth Symphony – a tragic statement damning the tyrant.

of international standing, who wrote all forms of classical music and invented new ones, incorporated the unique sounds and rhythms of jazz, blues, Negro spirituals and ragtime. America has also produced some of the greatest orchestras in the world today.

Another significant and probably unique aspect of American musical life was, and still is, the willingness to take great risks with music, encouraging new and innovative work. Composers felt free to experiment with music, away from the symphonic traditions of Europe and the fear that their music would be banned by oppressive political regimes. This sense of freedom was very attractive to composers, who more and more looked to America as a new stimulus for their work: Dvořák, Schoenberg, Stravinsky, Holst, Bartók, and many others are examples of this.

It was at the turn of the century that American composers found their own distinctive character in music. The first composer to become well known was Charles Ives (1874–1954). He was an insurance salesman who composed music in his spare time, not expecting to make any money out of it. His compositions have been affectionately described as sounding like 'walking down the street, hearing different sounds coming out of each doorway', a vivid way of capturing his use of two keys at the same time. His father, who was a band master, would get him to whistle a melody in one key and play the piano accompaniment in another, telling him that this was to stretch his ears. Some of his music is extremely complex to perform –

*Left* Dimitri Shostakovich

*Below* Aaron Copland

his Fourth Symphony needs four conductors to keep the players together. His Third Symphony is very melodic, and won him the Pulitzer Prize in 1947.

Aaron Copland (1900–90) wanted his music to have a distinctly American sound, so he used jazz and folk idioms. When he first presented his Organ Symphony to the American people a famous conductor remarked: 'If he can write like that at twenty-three, in five years he'll be ready to commit murder.' He trained in Paris for a while with Nadia Boulanger, eventually returning to New York, where he was known for his music for the stage, films and concert hall, and as a spokesman for his fellow composers. He used folk songs in his music because he wanted it to appeal to a wide audience – as in *Fanfare for the Common Man* (1942).

*Right* Elliott Carter

When Charles Ives' Third Symphony won the Pulitzer Prize in 1947, forty-two years after he had composed it, he told the awards committee, 'Prizes are for boys – I'm grown up!' and gave the $500 away.

One of his most famous orchestral works is the suite *El Salon Mexico* (1936), which was inspired by a visit to Mexico in 1932. It is written for a large orchestra, including percussion instruments used in Latin-American dance bands. He also wrote ballet music: *Appalachian Spring* and *Billy the Kid* are perhaps the best known. In *Billy the Kid* there is an orchestral representation of a gun fight. He wrote a clarinet concerto which was recorded by the legendary clarinetist, Benny Goodman. With his three symphonies he hoped to get away from being labelled a 'folk-inspired' composer – the Third Symphony, for instance, premiered by the Boston Symphony Orchestra in 1946, reflects the problems of war.

George Gershwin (1898–1937), famous for his popular songs and Broadway musicals, used popular music in his 'classical' scores for symphony orchestra. The most famous of these are *Rhapsody in Blue*, *An American in Paris* and the opera, *Porgy and Bess*. His songs display an inexhaustible ability to write unforgettable melodies. Unlike the other American musical writers, Gershwin was probably the only one apart from Bernstein to cross over successfully into the concert hall.

One of the expatriate composers to make a striking contribution to the use of percussion instruments was the Frenchman, Edgar Varèse (1883–1965), who emigrated to America in 1915. Interviewed by the press he said, 'We also need new instruments very badly – musicians should take up this question in deep earnest with the help of machinery specialists.' He worked with Maurice Martenot, who invented the ondes martenot in 1928. In America, he wrote *Amerique*

George Gershwin took lessons from various composers – Ravel and Stravinsky among others – so that he might improve his technical skills. In Hollywood, he became friends with Schoenberg and they played tennis together. He asked Schoenberg if he would teach him, to which he replied, 'I would only make you a bad Schoenberg and you are such a good Gershwin.'

*'I refuse to submit myself only to sounds that have already been heard.'*

Edgar Varèse

Leonard Bernstein

(1918–21) for large orchestra with a huge percussion section. It requires nine percussionists and two timpanists. In 1928 he wrote *Ionisation*, which was one of the first Western works written for percussion alone.

Elliott Carter (born 1908) was a close associate of Ives and studied at Harvard and in Paris with Nadia Boulanger. He writes very powerful and dramatic orchestral music – Variations for Orchestra, the Piano Concerto, and Double Concerto for Harpsichord, Piano and Two Chamber Orchestras.

It is said of Leonard Bernstein (1918–1990) that he could 'enter the Hall of Fame on the strength of one work, his Broadway musical, *West Side Story*', which is an updating of Shakespeare's *Romeo and Juliet*. His break as a conductor came in 1943, when Bruno Walter fell ill just before a concert and Bernstein took his place at short notice. After this, he became a world famous conductor as well as a composer.

It was in this atmosphere of freedom of expression that John Cage, Milton Babbitt, Morton Feldman, Earle Brown and Christian Wolff and many avant garde composers made their new and unique discoveries.

Australia, too, has emerged as an important force in orchestral music, with the music of Percy Grainger (1882–1961) and Malcolm Williamson (born 1921).

Percy Grainger staged his wedding at the Hollywood Bowl at a concert in front of 20,000 people, and bequeathed his skeleton to the University of Melbourne for preservation and possible display. A pianist-composer, he wrote an orchestral work out of the English Morris dance tune, 'Country Gardens', which was a great success for him. He collected English folk songs and, although his music is thought of as being quite lighthearted, he also wrote serious pieces. He once said of 'Country Gardens': 'I think of turnips when I play it.'

Malcolm Williamson (born 1931) is currently Master of the Queen's Music. He has written a lot of music for children. His love of jazz is heard in his Piano Concerto. He is also an organist and has written many compositions for the instrument. His opera, *The Violins of Saint-Jacques* is so tuneful it was once described as 'the thinking man's South Pacific'.

In Vienna in the early 1900s, a group of composers, the most notable of whom was Arnold Schoenberg (1874–1951), were busily experimenting with sound, eventually arriving at

Percy Grainger was a very athletic man and would often run from one concert to the next. During a concert tour in Africa, he misjudged the distance to the next venue. The audience had taken their seats and he was still nowhere in sight. His friends took some binoculars and looked out at the horizon, where they saw a cloud of dust. As it cleared, they could see a band of Zulu warriors heading for the township, with Grainger jogging along beside them. When they all arrived, Grainger demanded seats for the Zulus – but he had to accept that was impossible, because their admission would have led to him being deported immediately.

a whole new and abstract technique of writing music called atonality. This dreaded word wipes the smile off most faces because it seems to mean 'difficult', 'untuneful' and 'complicated'.

Since the dawn of mankind, we have learnt to understand music which sets up the melody and makes it sound secure to us. When we hear a melody by Mozart, it has a strong shape – we have a sense of where it's going and how it will end. Unlike this, an atonal melody challenges us by being unpredictable, which is exciting because we don't know what's going to happen next.

The increased use of percussive sounds and dissonance (clashing notes) in this music was at first unpalatable. It is interesting now to note that the reaction to it at the time was no different from that to all major changes in the history of music. Beethoven's and Wagner's music was also thought to be untuneful at first. People complained in the same way, saying 'This isn't music.'

This new system of harmony was championed by Schoenberg. His work, together with that of his friends and followers, especially Anton Webern (1883–1945) and Alban Berg (1885–1935), is known as the Second Viennese School (the 'first' Viennese school being Mozart, Haydn, Beethoven and Schubert.) Schoenberg also pioneered a new structural system for writing music based on a series of notes, 'Serial Music'.

This is a mathematical formula for writing music, based on a group of elements placed in a certain order or series. Schoenberg's aim in his serial compositions was to get away from all suggestion of tonal patterns of sounds. Alban Berg also applied serial technique to large orchestral works such as his Violin Concerto, using it less strictly than Schoenberg, while Webern wrote miniatures for full orchestra, using serial

Arnold Schoenberg

*Expressionism*: the term was borrowed from a group of painters: Picasso, Kandinsky and Klee. It was meant to denote a change from the 'impressions' gained from the outer world to 'expressions of the inner self' – a casting off of all rules in order to win complete freedom for musical expression. Schoenberg's *Erwartung*, *Die Glückliche Hand* and *Pierrot Lunaire* are all expressionist works.

technique for the rhythm as well as the melody and harmony. His Five Pieces For Orchestra (op.10) are extremely short, some of them less than one minute in length. By the end of his life, Webern had serialised all aspects of his music, making it a totally mathematical process without any direct emotional inspiration.

Webern was shot dead by mistake by an American soldier in 1945 while visiting his daughters in the mountains near Salzburg. After this he was hero-worshipped by his fellow composers and a new cult of 'minimalism' sprung up.

John Cage was born in 1912 in Los Angeles and studied with Schoenberg. He has written a piece called *Silence*, which consists of four minutes and thirty-three seconds of silence, the idea being that the music is created by the sounds provided by the natural environment at the time – that is, during the silence. Obviously, it is never the same twice and relies totally on the element of chance. *HPSCHD* (1967) is

*'The function of Avant garde is like fashion – self-destructive so that it can be replaced by a new collection.'*

Pierre Boulez, 1969

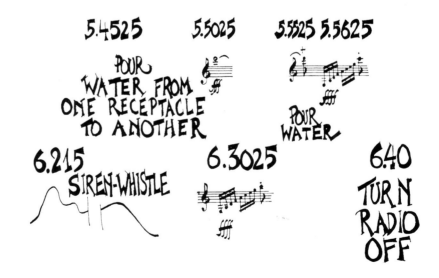

John Cage's Water Music

written for seven harpsichords and between one and fifty-one tape machines. *Imaginary Landscape* is for four radios. *0'00* is for any musician, playing anything, in any way.

John Cage said of himself in 1982, 'Schoenberg said I would never be able to compose because I have no ear for music. He said, "You'll always come to a wall and you won't be able to go through." I said, "Well then, I'll beat my head against that wall," and I quite literally began hitting things, and developed a music of percussion that involves noises.'

Living in a machine age as we do, electricity has inevitably taken its place in music and the electronic orchestra emerged, pioneered by Pierre Schaeffer (born 1910). He did not use direct electronic sounds but used machines to alter existing sounds, recording sounds from everyday life (saucepans, trains, voices) on disc, until the tape recorder became available in the early 1950s.

The Frenchman, Olivier Messaien (born 1908), experimented by using birdsong in his music, going out into the countryside and writing down the notes the birds were singing. He worked as an organist as a young man, and therefore wrote a lot of organ music up to about 1939. Having been taken prisoner by the Germans during the Second World War, he was repatriated on grounds of poor health and, on arriving home, started concentrating on orchestral and piano music. His *Quartet for the End of Time* was written in a concentration camp in 1940. Scored for clarinet, violin, cello and piano, it was first performed in the camp by himself and three fellow prisoners.

His ecstatic Turangalîla Symphony is one of the longest works in the orchestral repertoire. It is in ten movements and lasts ninety minutes, and was first performed in Boston on 2 December 1949, conducted by Leonard Bernstein. 'Turanga'

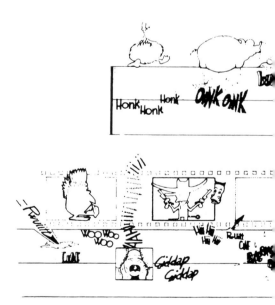

At the turn of the century, Nadia Boulanger was working in Paris, teaching many young composers. She was a composer herself and an inspirational teacher, and is said to have had an encyclopaedic knowledge of music and its history. She stopped composing when her sister, Lili (the first woman to win the Prix de Rome (1913)), died tragically at the age of twenty-four.

*Left* Olivier Messaien

*Below* Example of a graphic score – *Stripsody* by Cathy Berberian

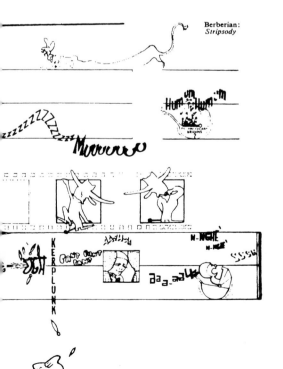

means 'galloping time' and 'lîla' love, or life itself, so once again, love and death are put together. It requires a large orchestra and includes the piano extensively throughout, and many percussion instruments. In this symphony, he proudly introduces the new electronic instrument, the ondes martenot. Although he uses it frequently in his other works as well, it has never gained a permanent place in the orchestra. Its inventor called it 'Martenot Waves' because it can swoop up and down.

Messaien has become very influential as a teacher, working at the Paris Conservatoire, teaching many composers who were themselves to become extremely important – most notably Pierre Boulez (born 1925) and Karlheinz Stockhausen (born 1928). Between them they were to take Schaeffer's ideas further, encouraged by Messaien.

These composers work with pure sounds, both pitched and unpitched, creating them in a purely electronic way using tape recorders, synthesisers and computers. Boulez has tried out electronic ideas, using serial techniques as the foundation for the music – and has now built his own electronic studio in Paris, as Stockhausen has done in Cologne.

Like John Cage's music, a piece by Stockhausen never sounds the same twice because he uses the improvisatory element of chance, known as 'aleatory' music.

The Italian composer Luciano Berio (born 1925) follows the Stockhausen/Boulez school of the later 1950s, using these techniques with voices to create a very individual style.

In all this music, there is a desire on the composer's part to involve the musician playing the music in a more creative way – the player's personal interpretation becomes part of the composition. More often than not it is left to the player to decide exactly how the music should be played, within certain

151

guidelines set by the composer. Notes are played 'at random' within a given framework. The player is frequently required to improvise to create a sense that something unprepared could happen. In order to express these new ideas and sounds, a new system of notation is required. Each composer tends to find his own way of expressing the music on the page. A device called 'proportional notation' has been invented to express the shape of the music in a drawing. The scores become detailed graphic drawings – works of art in their own right.

Stockhausen abandons notation altogether, writing a 'text score', explaining in words how the music should be played. In one piece he instructs the musicians to starve themselves for four days and nights before the performance of the music.

Since the end of the 1960s, there has been a move back to simplicity with the rise of minimalism (from Webern) in the USA, with, among others, Terry Riley (born 1913), Philip Glass (born 1937) and Steve Reich (born 1936). The signs of this are seen earlier in the music of the Greek composer Xenakis (born 1922) and the Hungarian, Ligeti (born 1923). Composers now talk of 'landscapes of sound' and 'clusters of tones'.

Contemporary composers work in a mixture of styles. The search for new sounds continues using different combinations of instruments to create unusual sonorities. Harrison Birtwistle, for example, uses a mixture of woodwind, electronic tape, and strings in *Medusa* (1967).

Lately, there has been a revival of more tonal ideas through the music of Arthur Schnittke, Arvo Pärt and Michael Berkeley. And composers continue to write music, as they always have done, about subjects which are close to their hearts, working with contemporary writers and poets. For example, Michael Berkeley's oratorio based on Ian McEwan's

### GOLD DUST

live completely alone for four days
without food
in complete silence, without much movement
sleep as little as necessary
think as little as possible

after four days, late at night,
without conversation beforehand
play single sounds

WITHOUT THINKING which you are playing

close your eyes
just listen

Stockhausen's *Gold Dust*, an example of a text score

poem *Or Shall We Die?*, expresses a woman's desperation and feelings for her children after a nuclear disaster.

The symphony as a form of music for the orchestra lives on through the work of contemporary symphonists such as the Polish composer, Witold Lutoslawski (born 1913), whose Third Symphony was commissioned by Sir Georg Solti for the Chicago Symphony Orchestra and first performed in 1983. It uses a full orchestra of 105 players, including a large percussion section which features the tuned keyboard percussion – vibraphone, marimba, xylophone, and bells, as well as a piano. It is in two movements but should be performed all the way through without a break. Only part of the score is conducted. There are ad lib sections, and the note values are approximate, so music written in the score for different instruments will not necessarily be heard exactly together – it is made up of episodes of sound.

Lutoslawski remained in Poland during the Second World War and worked in radio communications. When the Nazis invaded Poland and took over all the orchestras, insisting that only German music be played, he took to the basement cafés and played piano duets with his friend Andrej Panufnik, arranging over 200 works for piano duet, most of which were lost in the Warsaw uprising in 1944. After the war, his First Symphony caused a great scandal, was banned by the authorities in 1949 because it didn't conform to the regulations for music, and wasn't performed again until 1959. The Polish government eventually decorated him for his work because he wrote music for 'social need', especially songs for children.

It was after he heard John Cage's Piano Concerto that he realised the full potential of the Avant Garde ideas. He believes that the art of composing for orchestra is dying out and has very strong views about this. He believes that new instruments

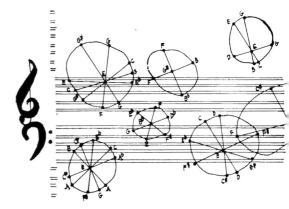

Extract from John Cage's Piano Concerto, an example of proportional notation

Witold Lutoslawski, Sir Georg Solti and the Chicago Symphony Orchestra in 1983, at the first performance of the composer's Third Symphony

Arnold Dolmetsch (1858–1940) made it his life's work to restore and repair early instruments. He then started making new models of early instruments – lutes, clavichords, harpsichords. He was the first to make the plastic recorder, used by children in schools everywhere. Through his work he saved many early instruments from extinction and inspired instrument makers since, giving us the opportunity to hear early music played on original instruments, in an authentic way.

must be invented if orchestral music is to continue.

So what has happened to the orchestra? Many new symphony orchestras have been founded this century and the number of players in these orchestras is now standardised at a hundred or over. Many small chamber orchestras have emerged to perform early music where such large numbers of musicians are not required, and there is new interest in presenting 'authentic' orchestras made up of the exact number and types of instruments used by past composers when their music was originally performed. This interest in authenticity has also inspired instrument makers not only to repair early instruments, but also to build copies of them so that music of earlier centuries can be played today on replicas of the instruments for which it was originally intended.

Now a truly international business, conductors, composers and musicians go all over the world to work. Never before have there been so many opportunities to hear orchestral music.

# The Percussion

Each step in the development of orchestral music seems to coincide with the creation or improvement of a group of instruments. This century began with new ideas about rhythm that created harsher and more violent sounds than ever before. This, in turn, led to an increased use of percussion instruments, many of which came from the East and Latin America. The orchestra, ever bigger and more powerful, accommodated these changes and made a large percussion section a standard feature. These instruments not only helped the new, stronger rhythms, but they also gave new colour to orchestral sound. Previously, percussion instruments, specifically drums, had been used simply to emphasise rhythm and to 'cap' a climax in the music.

The word 'percussion' is used to describe any instrument which is played by shaking or striking it. They divide into two groups – those of definite pitch and those of indefinite pitch. Some are used for their rhythmic effects – drums, cymbals, triangle, tambourine, woodblock, maracas, claves and castanets. Others play melodies – glockenspiel, marimba, xylophone, celeste, vibraphone, tubular bells.

Percussion instruments have been around for a long time – nobody quite knows when the first drum was used. They come from all over the world, particularly from India, China, Latin America and Africa. And an orchestra's percussionist is expected to be able to play most of them, even if it means switching quickly from one to another during a performance.

It takes a great deal of courage to play a percussion instrument and the only way to play well is to have a strong sense of rhythm. After sitting silently, counting bar after bar, a

percussionist may have to come in with just one beat on a triangle – and if it's wrong, everyone knows. Playing percussion is also more than just 'hitting things'. There are many different sounds that can be made on any one instrument and learning to play them takes a lot of practice. A specialist may practise for two hours a day, concentrating at different times on soft notes, muffled notes, playing very quickly, or learning complicated rhythms. It is, however, very easy to get a recognisable note out of a percussion instrument – you just hit it.

There are many different types of beater and choosing the correct one is vital. It is not unusual for a conductor to question the percussionist on the choice of beaters if the sound is not right. Most contemporary composers, however, give detailed instructions on how the instruments should be played to achieve the correct sound for the piece.

Most percussionists begin by playing drums. The orchestra's timpanist usually only plays the kettledrums, whereas other percussion players are expected to play practically any combination of other percussion instruments, depending on the requirements of the piece.

### Timpani

The oldest member of the percussion family is the kettledrum or timpani. They are made by stretching a membrane of skin, or plastic, over a large copper bowl, which comes in four main sizes – 30ins, 28ins, 25ins and 23ins in diameter. There is also a very small timpani measuring 21ins across, but this is sometimes replaced by another drum such as the tom-tom. Modern timpani can be tuned by foot pedals to play around five notes. They are a great improvement on

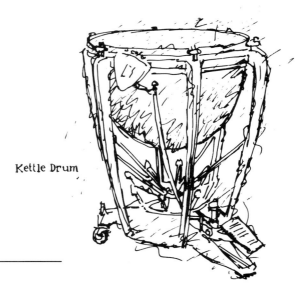

Kettle Drum

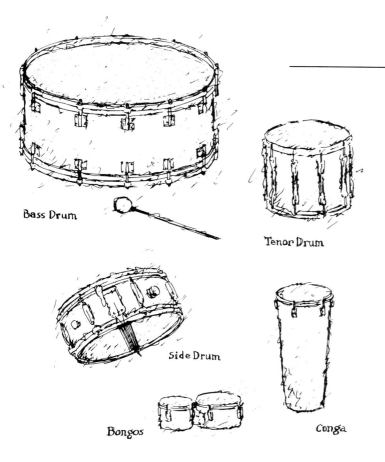

Bass Drum

Tenor Drum

Side Drum

Bongos

Conga

sticks or wire brushes; the lower skin has 'snares' – lengths of gut, wire or nylon – stretched across it which vibrate when the drum is hit, giving a dry, rattling sound. If the snares are not required, they can be loosened so that they don't vibrate.

### Tenor drum
At first glance, this looks like a deeper version of the side drum. It is, but it does not have snares.

### Bass drum
The bass drum is huge and impossible to miss at the back of the orchestra. It has two heads, like the side drum, but because of its size is usually suspended on a frame. It is struck with large, felt-covered beaters and makes a deep booming sound. It is also used to simulate thunder because of the rumbling noises it makes when rolled softly.

### Bongos
Single-headed, Latin-American drums that always come in pairs. They were originally played by hand not beater and held between the knees, although in the orchestra they are usually mounted on a stand and struck with wooden snare drumsticks.

### Conga Drum
Latin-American bass drum used regularly in the modern symphony orchestra.

those used in the Classical era, which were tuned by turning keys around the edge of the skin.

### Side Drum
The side drum or snare drum is so-called because it was, and still is, carried to the side when played in military bands. Like the timpani, it has been used by composers for a long time, particularly in opera.

A side drum has two 'heads'. The top is the usual drum skin which is struck with wooden

### Tambourine

A hand-held 'drum' 10ins in diameter, with pairs of metal discs like small cymbals, which jangle around the edges. The tambourine, too, has been around for a long time – references to it can be found in the Bible. Usually struck with the hand or shaken, it is sometimes fixed to a stand so that the player can use sticks and beaters.

### Tom-tom

A small drum that can be tuned to approximate pitches if desired. The Chinese tom-tom has two heads, the Indian tom-tom only one. Like the bongos, they come in pairs, and are usually played with the hands and fingers.

### Tam-tam

A large gong, struck with felt-covered beaters. Like the bass drum, it cannot be missed at the back of the orchestra – it's the huge metal disc suspended on a frame.

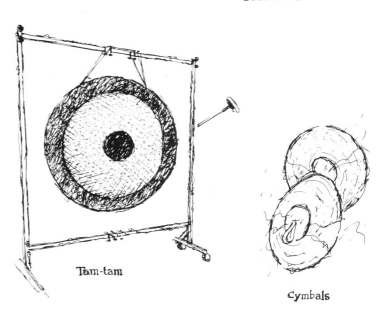

Tam-tam

Cymbals

### Cymbals

Originally from Turkey, cymbals come in three varieties: suspended, hi-hat and hand-held. The largest and by far the loudest are the hand-held ones, which are cup-shaped metal discs with a leather handle in the middle. The suspended cymbal is held on a stand or frame so the player can strike it with sticks or beaters. The hi-hat cymbals are more commonly found in jazz bands as part of the drum kit. Mounted on a metal rod, they jump up and down by use of a foot pedal.

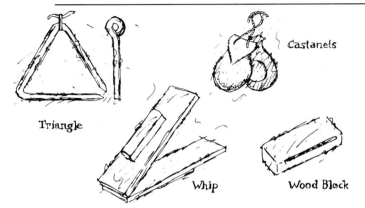

Triangle

Castanets

Whip

Wood Block

### The triangle

A triangular-shaped metal bar with one open corner, this comes in several sizes and is beaten with various types of small metal rod. Again of Turkish origin, it was used a great deal in early opera, but was not used regularly in the orchestra until Beethoven's time.

### Castanets

Two hollow wooden shells, held in one hand, which are used for Spanish flamenco dancing. They have been around for hundreds of years and are thought to be of Mediterranean origin. They are now used to give a Spanish feel to orchestral music and are generally mounted for the percussionist on a wooden board.

### Whip

Two pieces of smooth wood which, when slapped together, make a sound like a whip. The Europeans call it a whip, the Americans a slapstick. It is usually used to emphasise a sudden, loud chord.

### Woodblock

Blocks of wood hollowed out in the middle, these come in up to five sizes, which, although they are unpitched, do have different sounds.

### Guiro

Oval-shaped wooden object with notches like a washboard that comes originally from Latin America. It is played by rubbing a stick or metal fork against it.

### Ratchet

A football rattle

### Maracas

Latin-American instruments that usually come in pairs. They consist of hollow wooden shells filled with seeds that rattle when shaken.

### Claves

Also Latin American, claves are simply two hollow sticks which are tapped together.

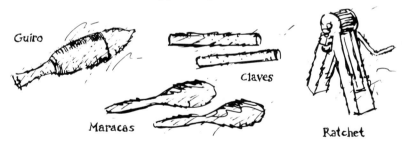

Guiro

Claves

Maracas

Ratchet

### Tubular bells

Eighteen hollow metal tubes of varying sizes, suspended on a frame. They are struck with a leather mallet, making a sound like church bells.

## Glockenspiel

In German, 'Glockenspiel' means 'play with bells' and the term is the one most commonly used to describe orchestral bells – thirty steel plates of varying sizes arranged like a keyboard and played with wooden or metal beaters.

## Celeste

Invented by Mustel in 1886, this is the keyboard version of the Glockenspiel, and is shaped like an upright piano, with a pedal and felt hammers that strike the metal bars.

## Xylophone

Like the glockenspiel, this sounds an octave higher than is written. It also looks like the glockenspiel, only its bars are wooden not metal, hence its name, which comes from the Greek for 'wood sound'. Because of its quieter sound, metal tubes under the wooden bars help the sound to resonate.

## Marimba

A direct descendant of the xylophone, the marimba sounds an octave lower. Its wooden bars, usually made of rose wood, span four octaves and make a deep, mellow sound. First used in the orchestra around 1950.

## Vibraphone

Invented in America, this looks like a large glockenspiel, with vertical resonating tubes underneath each metal bar. Each tube has an electric fan at the top which helps the sound to vibrate

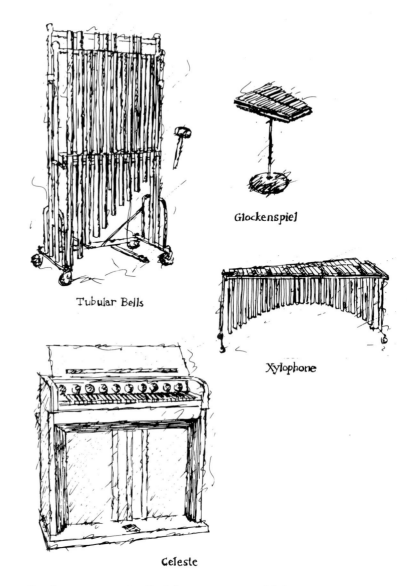

Tubular Bells

Glockenspiel

Xylophone

Celeste

– the fans are controlled by a motor, which can be adjusted to blow air out at different speeds. Played using rubber mallets, it differs from the glockenspiel, xylophone, marimba and celeste because it can make vibrato and tremolo sounds.

# The Piano

*'We're going to feature an instrument which doesn't normally appear in the orchestra, except in modern times, the piano, which we devote a whole programme to because I like to play it.'*
Dudley Moore

With over seven octaves and eighty-eight keys, a modern piano can play a wider range of notes than any other orchestral instrument, although the piccolo player might claim to be able to play higher, and the tuba player lower. Out-playing the piano's range, though, depends entirely on the player's ability to reach these notes, which are not necessarily natural to the instrument.

The piano's range has not always been this wide. Early pianos neither sounded nor looked like the instrument seen today and it is only in the last 150 years that anything resembling the modern instrument has been used.

Several things have contributed to the piano's evolution: the constant search for new sounds which first led instrument makers in the 1700s to experiment with existing keyboard instruments; changes in musical fashions that necessitated a louder instrument – the arrival of the large concert hall, for instance; the Romantic era, with its emphasis on the expression of strong passions, and finally virtuoso pianists and composers, who, because of its increasingly beautiful sound, pushed it to the limits of its expressive qualities.

The first working piano was built around 1700 by the Italian harpsichord maker and keeper of the instruments at the Medici Court in Florence, Bartolomeo Cristofori. The idea to create a keyboard instrument which could play loudly and softly by varying finger pressure on the keys probably came from a desire to combine in one instrument the gentle expressive qualities of the clavichord (whose loudness could be varied by finger pressure) with the more declamatory sounds of the harpsichord.

At first, the piano was much the same size as the harpsichord, having a keyboard of only three and a half octaves, and from the outside could have been mistaken for one. It

*Above* The harpsichord, a forerunner of the piano (*below*)

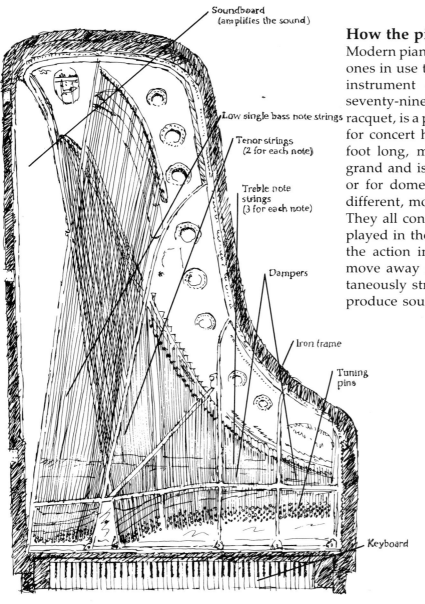

Soundboard
(amplifies the sound)

Low single bass note strings

Tenor strings
(2 for each note)

Treble note
strings
(3 for each note)

Dampers

Iron frame

Tuning
pins

Keyboard

## How the piano works

Modern pianos come in different sizes. The main ones in use today are the concert grand, a huge instrument – nine foot long and weighing seventy-nine stone – which, like the new tennis racquet, is a power machine. It is reserved mostly for concert halls. The baby grand is about five foot long, makes a softer sound than the full grand and is therefore ideal for chamber music or for domestic use; and the upright is just a different, more compact shape.

They all contain the same components and are played in the same way. Pressing the keys sets the action in motion, causing the dampers to move away from the strings, which are simultaneously struck with a hammer and vibrate to produce sound.

The frame on a modern piano must support even heavier strings whose tension is greater than ever before. A modern grand uses one large string per note for the bass, two strings per note for the middle range and three per note for the top. The string tension is about 180–200lbs per string, making a total tension of eighteen tons.

A modern piano can cost anything from £500 for a second-hand upright to £40,000 for a Steinway concert grand.

had the same delicate, decorated wooden case to hold the strings stretched on a wooden frame inside, and the same spindly legs. The keys were the same colour as those of the harpsichord – the reverse of the modern piano. Indeed, the early pianos were called 'Gravicembalo col piano e forte' (Harpsichord with a soft and loud), hence the name it was eventually given – the pianoforte. The important difference between the two was the way in which the strings were made to produce the sound. Instead of being plucked, as on a harpsichord, a piano's strings were struck with a hammer, making the sound instantly more robust.

Cristofori also understood that to make a louder sound the new instrument would need heavier strings. Instead of using one string per note like the harpsichord, he used two. The hammers were initially quite hard and the mechanism used to make them strike the strings quite simple and not very accurate. It took time for the hammers to complete the action of striking the strings. As a result, it was not possible to play particularly fast and every note played was followed by a dull thud as the hammer returned to its position.

Since 'touch' is vital to successful virtuoso performance, the makers set about redesigning the action to make it lighter and swifter. Sebastian Erard finally discovered the solution with his 'double-escapement' action, which enabled a key to be played repeatedly without returning to its position of rest.

Details of Cristofori's piano spread throughout Europe. An Italian, Maffei, published an account which was translated into German in 1722. This was taken up by the organ builder Gottfried Silbermann, who promptly made two pianos identical to Cristofori's in 1726. Maffei's diagrams, however, had been drawn from memory and were not accurate. As a result, Silbermann's first attempts were a disaster – Bach, when he

It was the French who first used the piano in the orchestra in the late 1800s. And they used it as an orchestral instrument in the true sense – placed in the middle of the orchestra rather than out in front. As an orchestral instrument it can be used to fill in harmonies or to play solos. It can be used as a percussion instrument, complementing the xylophone, marimba or vibraphone, with its bass notes used to play with the timpani. Or, just to prove its versatility, it can play arpeggios like a harp.

Classical piano technique is not only used by classical pianists — many famous jazz pianists were classically trained, although there is a special technique for playing jazz. It's said that Oscar Peterson plays Bach for two hours every morning — and so does Dudley Moore. It is best to have a piano with a bright tone when playing jazz, and you must have the ability to improvise. There are a few characteristic techniques, such as wide leaps with the left hand, and the use of the thumb as a kind of pivot, to play middle harmony notes. Whatever the style of playing, all pianists need fingers like mini-athletes, which takes a lot of practice — slow practice.

was shown one, was unimpressed, finding the touch too heavy and the treble sound too flimsy. Silbermann made modifications of his own and when one of his new instruments turned up at the Court of Frederick the Great, Bach gave it his full approval. After Cristofori and Silbermann, keyboard building took hold in Vienna and London, France and America.

The piano arrived in England in 1752, when Samuel Crisp purchased one from a monk in Rome and brought it to London. One of Silbermann's pupils, Zumpe, came to London in 1760 and developed his square piano, which became a fashionable domestic instrument.

The most important developments in English piano building were made by John D. Broadwood between 1772 and 1776. Still struggling with the problem of the piano's action, Broadwood conducted experiments with the help of the British Museum to determine the optimum point to strike a string with a hammer to produce an even sound – it was discovered to be a ninth of the way along the string.

The first notable appearance of the piano in London was at the Covent Garden theatre in 1767. Charles Dibdin used one to accompany a singer. The first public performance for solo piano was given in Dublin by Henry Walsh in 1768 and two weeks later in London, on 2 June 1768, by J.C. Bach.

In Vienna, Stein (1728–92) solved the problem of producing a smooth piano action in 1777 and his instrument was taken up by Mozart. But the instrument still only had five octaves.

The piano became the most popular household musical instrument throughout northern Europe. It was even made in different shapes for use in the parlour – square, upright, giraffe, and even pyramid-shaped. The square shape finally lost its popularity with the arrival of the upright, which was first made by the Americans, Hawkins of Philadelphia, in 1800, and in London from 1811 by Robert Wornum.

The ever-increasing size of concert halls meant a louder instrument was needed. Makers started using thick, high-tension strings, which in turn meant a stronger frame was needed to support them. In 1825 the iron frame was first used by Hawkins in America, followed by Broadwood's in England.

Another addition in the early 1800s were the pedals. The soft pedal (*una corda*) restricts the level of sound by moving the keyboard and hammers sideways so that one string of

Up to a certain point a piano is easy to play in that you just have to touch a key to make an accurate note. But getting the touch right is crucial. The legendary pianist, Vladimir Horowitz, remarked that the piano is difficult to play because you need to make it sing and this is not something it does naturally. Getting a good tone is the most difficult part – the rest is application.

*Above right* The piano duet

*Above left* The giraffe piano

each note is left unstruck; the sustaining pedal (often wrongly called the 'loud' pedal) removes the dampers from the strings so that the note continues to sound after the fingers have been removed from the keys. There is sometimes a third pedal, the *sostenuto* pedal, which is an ingenious device that enables the player to hold over a limited selection of notes.

A more recent, important manufacturer was Heinrich Steinweg, who, in the middle of the nineteenth century, set up Steinway & Sons in New York. He discovered the technique of 'over-stringing', a method of spreading the strings over the sound board to produce a louder, more resonant tone. This technique had been used on the clavichord – but it had a significant effect when applied to the piano. By 1860 the piano had grown to seven octaves, almost its modern size.

# Composers and the Piano

Before the invention of the piano, composers tended not to specify which keyboard instrument should be used because there was little difference between the sound of one keyboard and another. The first music to be published that leaves no doubt as to which keyboard instrument it was written for was the *Sonate da Cembalo di piano e forte dello volgarmente di marelletti* (little hammers) by Lodovico Giustini, published in Florence in 1732.

But the piano did not take over from the harpsichord overnight – it was not widely available initially and the earliest models, as already explained, had teething problems. Johann Sebastian Bach's sons did much to promote the piano, particularly C. P. E. Bach, who, in 1780, wrote sonatas especially for the piano, using instruments with a keyboard of a maximum of five and a half octaves. His music was the first to reveal its special sound qualities. The hesitant steps to find an individual style of composition for the piano can be seen by the fact that his Double Concerto for Harpsichord and Piano (1788) treats both instruments in an identical fashion.

Gradually, the piano took over the 'continuo' function from the harpsichord. Haydn would sit at the piano to conduct his London Symphonies (1794) – in the same position in front of the orchestra as the musical director using a harpsichord had occupied. On one occasion, he realised he hadn't touched the keyboard once during the performance. At the end of the symphony he suddenly broke into a burst of playing so as not to disappoint his audience, who had been informed in the concert posters, 'Mr Haydn will reside at the piano.'

Beethoven said the reason why Mozart's piano music re-

The piano can be played by two people, one person or even one hand. C. P. E. Bach wrote keyboard pieces for right or left hand alone. The most famous one-handed pianist was the Austrian Paul Wittgenstein (1887–1961) who lost his right arm in the First World War. Since he wanted to resume his career as a concert pianist he let composers know that he needed new music for the left hand and in 1930 Maurice Ravel wrote a concerto for him.

quired such a light touch was that he learned his keyboard technique on a harpsichord and played the piano in the same style. The English and French instruments, on the other hand, had deeper keys, requiring a stronger touch.

Mozart wrote a vast amount of beautiful keyboard music, both sonatas and concertos, which are very revealing about the size and power of the piano he played. His Concerto in E flat K.271, written in 1777, was originally intended for the harpsichord, but later that year in Munich he tried it out on, as he put it, 'a wretched pianoforte'. The first piano to impress Mozart was made by Stein in Vienna that same year. It had a better tone and smoother action.

Beethoven, by comparison, was a notorious 'piano smasher'. This was caused partly perhaps by the frustration of his deafness, and partly because his compositions demanded such big sounds from the instrument. He knew all the piano makers in Vienna at the time, but it was the London piano makers, Broadwood's, who were to make an instrument especially for him. Thomas Broadwood wrote:

> It was in August 1817 I had the pleasure of seeing Beethoven in Vienna. He was then so unwell, his table supported as many vials of medicine as it did sheets of music paper, and his clothes so scattered about the room in the manner of an invalid that I was not surprised when I called on him by appointment to take him out to dine with us at the Prater, to find him declare after he had one foot in the carriage that he found himself too unwell to dine out – and he retreated upstairs. I saw him several times after that at his own house and he was kind enough to play with me, but he was so deaf and unwell.

When Thomas Broadwood returned to London he sent Beethoven a piano – a six-octave grand with a Spanish mahogany

Extract from the original score of Beethoven's Piano Sonata No. 26

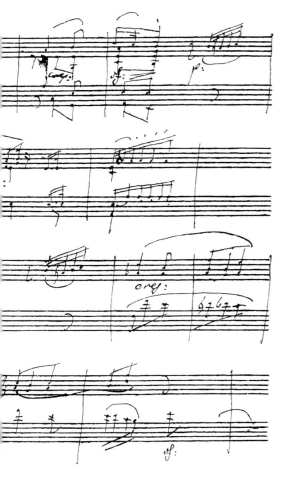

case inlaid with marquetry and ormolu, and brass carrying handles in the shape of laurel wreaths. Despatched in January 1818 by sea to Trieste, it then travelled 200 miles overland on a cart to Vienna, not arriving there until May because it had been held up at customs, who demanded duty be paid on it. When it did finally arrive, it was still in tune.

Beethoven was delighted with it – he even used to take it on holiday with him. The Broadwood family was well connected in London musical circles, and Beethoven relied on commissions from London orchestras for income, so he wrote an extremely warm letter of thanks, praising the fine qualities of the piano and promising to send 'the first fruits' of composition on it to London. There is no proof that this ever happened.

Ludwig Rellstab, the poet, visited Beethoven just after the piano was delivered and wrote the following account of the meeting. Hoping that Beethoven would play the piano for him, he went up to the Broadwood and played a chord on it:

> I softly struck a chord with the left hand; but he did not seem to hear it. In a minute or two he turned round to me and said, 'It is a beautiful piano. It was sent to me as a present from London. It is a handsome present and has a fine tone.' Looking at me and putting out his hand towards the keyboard, but without turning round, he struck a chord softly. Never will another fill me with such melancholy. He had a C major in the right hand and struck B in the bass and, looking at me, he steadily repeated the wrong chord several times that I might hear the sweet tone of the instrument; yet the greatest musician on earth did not perceive the discord.

This piano suffered a beating from Beethoven. His friend Stumpff said in 1824, on seeing the wrecked piano, 'There was no sound left in the treble and broken strings were mixed up like a thorn bush in a gale.'

The range of expression in Beethoven's piano music shows just what the developing instrument was capable of. With the arrival of Romanticism and the virtuoso composer-player, ever greater demands were made of it.

Franz Liszt was the most famous, and passionate, of Romantic keyboard composers, modelling himself on Paganini's style of virtuoso playing. Apart from being a highly innovative composer, whose orchestral music inspired other great composers such as Wagner, Richard Strauss and Debussy, he was a dynamic and astonishing pianist who stunned and shocked wherever he played.

Born in Hungary, Liszt, like Mozart, was a child prodigy. He gave his first public performance when he was eleven and made his London debut at the age of twelve. He believed that any piece of music could sound just as good, if not better, when played on the piano. His great showmanship covered a lot of wrong notes but the audience did not seem to mind. The *Musical World* described him in 1841:

> We walk through this world in the midst of so many wonders that our senses become indifferent to the most amazing things: light and life, the ocean, the forest, the voice and flight of the pigmy lark, are unheeded commonplaces; and it is only when some comet, some giant, tiger-tamer, some new Niagara, some winged being appears, that our obdurate facilities are roused into consciousness that miracles do exist. Of the miracle genus is Liszt, the Polyphemus of the pianoforte – the Aurora Borealis of musical effulgence – the Niagara of thundering harmonies!

Liszt treated the piano as if it were a self-contained orchestra. Many of the pieces he played on it were transcriptions of

Liszt visited London in 1840 and puzzled the musical public by announcing 'Pianoforte Recitals'. This now commonly accepted term had never been used before, and people asked, 'What does he mean? How can anyone recite on the piano?' At these recitals, Liszt, after performing a piece set down in the programme, would get down off the platform and walk around in the audience, talking to his friends with, it was reported, 'the gracious condescension of a prince', until such time as he felt like playing the next piece on the programme.

orchestral pieces from Bach to Berlioz. Audiences adored him, particularly the women, for his flamboyance. His musical contemporaries were sometimes insulted by him showing off with their music, but still could not help but admire him.

Liszt was a great friend of Robert Schumann (1810–56), who also composed some of the greatest piano works in the Romantic period. The son of a bookseller and publisher, he played the piano from an early age and started composing in his teens. But his life was to be a struggle and end in tragedy. When he was sixteen his sister committed suicide. His father then became ill and died. Torn between publishing and being a concert pianist, he continued composing and writing for a new music magazine, which he founded and ran for ten years.

## Practising the Piano

A selection of instructions for keyboard playing from Schumann's *House Rules and Maxims for Young Musicians* (1848):

1 You must practise scales and other finger exercises assiduously. There are people, however, who think they may achieve great ends by doing this; for many years, for many hours, they practise mechanical exercises. That makes as much sense as trying to recite the alphabet faster and faster every day. Put your time to better use.

2 'Silent keyboards' have been invented; practise on them for a while just to see how useless they are. Silent people cannot teach us to speak.

3 Never play bad compositions, and never listen to them unless you absolutely have to.

4 Never strum along! Always play energetically and never fail to finish the piece you have begun.

5 Dragging and hurrying are equally great faults.

6 Try to play easy pieces well. It's better than playing difficult ones badly.

7 Always play as though the composer were present.

8 Don't be led astray by applause bestowed on great virtuosi. The applause of a great artist is more to be cherished than that of the majority.

9 Never lose an opportunity to practise on the organ. No instrument takes a swifter revenge on anything unclear in composition and playing.

10 Art was not created as a way to riches. Strive to become a true artist; the rest will take care of itself.

To improve his piano technique, Schumann invented a device to stretch the fourth finger of his right hand – a sort of sling mechanism. But it resulted in permanent damage to his hand, which ultimately forced him to give up virtuoso playing. This was one of many signs of his manic nature.

At the age of twenty-five, he fell in love with Clara Wieck, his piano teacher's daughter. Clara was, herself, an accomplished pianist and composer and became one of the leading pianists of her generation. Robert wrote all his music for her. Her father, however, objected vehemently to the relationship and for five years refused permission for the two to marry. He even took Schumann to court, first accusing him of being a drunkard and therefore unfit to marry, secondly on financial grounds.

But Robert and Clara eventually married and settled into a life that was at first one of perfect happiness. They each had their own music room with a piano. If they weren't practising, Schumann would read Goethe and Shakespeare with Clara and together they would study Bach. He wrote over one hundred songs in the first year of their marriage inspired by his love for her. They went on tour throughout Europe together, Clara playing the pieces Robert had written.

It was Liszt who introduced Schumann's music to the French by playing it in Paris and publishing articles about his work in the press. He also wrote about Clara and on one occasion asked her if she was pleased with his article. She asked, 'What made you say I practised with a black cat on each side of the pianoforte desk? You know that isn't true.' 'My dear Madam,' he replied, 'In order to make an article like that go down with the French public it must have something piquant about it.'

One of Schumann's best-known works, his Piano Concerto

*'It is impossible to communicate with Schumann. The man is hopeless. He doesn't talk at all.'*

Richard Wagner

'I started learning the piano when I was five. My piano teacher used to hit my fingers – I absolutely hated him, so after a year I'd had enough. The other boys went out to play football and I had to practise. I told my mother, 'I'm not playing piano anymore. Full stop.' A year later, we had our first singing lesson at school and a young boy accompanied on the piano very badly. I thought, I can do better than that. It was then that I realised that I wanted to play it. So I started again at seven and never stopped. I have never forgotten that singing lesson.'

Sir Georg Solti

'I started because there was a piano in the house. I used to crawl onto it when I was three. I loved sight-reading, and before I knew anything about harmony, I used to get music out of the library and try to read the black dots, wondering what on earth they were. I would pinch all my sister's music – a lot of Chopin, which I hated because I couldn't play it then, it was too difficult for me. Then I got interested in jazz because I wanted to make myself attractive to the opposite sex and it seemed this was the only way to achieve this.'

Dudley Moore

'I love the Schumann Piano Concerto and that's why we chose it for the series. I heard it as a kid on the radio at the Proms. It's a deceptive piece. He does these difficult arpeggios, relying on the finger, the one he tried to strengthen and, in doing so, crippled his hand.'

Dudley Moore

in A minor, was written for Clara. She gave the first performance of it in Dresden on 4 December 1845. The first movement
had been written in 1841 as a piece in its own right – a
Concert Fantasie. The concerto, unlike most of the passionate,
elaborate music being written during the Romantic period,
appears relatively simple in places. But, inspired as it was by
Clara, there is no doubt about the passion behind it and it is
now regarded as one of the most difficult concertos in the
piano repertoire.

In 1850 Schumann was appointed Director of Music in
Düsseldorf but he had little success as he was too inexperi-
enced a conductor. He began to suffer regularly from bouts
of serious depression – having in the past showed signs of
being unstable, particularly after intensive periods of composition, when he would withdraw into a nervous, exhausted
state for months.

In 1854, he tried to commit suicide by walking into the
Rhine. Not long afterwards, his condition became so bad he
was committed to a private asylum, where he spent the last
two years of his life. Clara was not allowed to see him because
of his insanity, although they wrote to each other throughout.
She was finally summoned to him just before he died.

Schumann wrote many articles supporting his fellow composers. When he heard Frédéric Chopin play (1810–49) he
said, 'Hats off, Gentlemen, a genius.' Chopin and Schumann
were born in the same year and met first at the Wiecks'
house. Chopin, although born in Poland, spent most of his
short life in Paris, where he became friends with Liszt and
Berlioz.

Most of Chopin's compositions were for the piano. A brilliant pianist, he was playing in public by the time he was eight,
and could improvise with ease. His main source of income

*'To me, Schumann's memory is holy. This noble, pure artist remains my ideal. I will hardly be privileged to love a better person.'*
Johannes Brahms

The score of the Schumann Piano Concerto was sold recently at Sotheby's in London for the sum of £400,000.

Schumann wrote to Clara just before they were married:

> 'I have at last had a chance of hearing Liszt's wonderful playing, which alternates between a fine frenzy and utter delicacy. But this would not be mine, my little Clara. Art, as we know it – you when you play, I when I compose – has an intimacy and charm that is worth more to me than all Liszt's splendid tinsel.'

Before he was married, Schumann went to Vienna in search of work which might improve his financial position and to see if Clara and he could live there, where she, too, might command higher fees. He went to visit Schubert's brother, a poor schoolteacher, and there found many of Schubert's unpublished works. He sent the manuscripts to a publisher, in the hope of raising money for Schubert's brother. Schubert's last symphony, 'The Great C Major', was among the scores. Schumann gave this to his friend and conductor, Mendelssohn, who gave the first performance in Leipzig in 1839 – eleven years after Schubert's death.

was from teaching the piano to wealthy young ladies, and playing in salons.

Liszt introduced Chopin to George Sands, a highly controversial woman who dressed like a man and had radical views on relationships. Chopin's involvement with her was a mixed blessing, for when they separated he was so distressed he hardly wrote any music at all and died two years later, aged only thirty-nine. Constantly ill, Berlioz remarked of him, 'He was dying all his life.'

Chopin's piano music is full of beautiful melodies – on one hand lyrical and romantic, on the other, strong and dramatic. His music for solo piano includes ballades, études, mazurkas, polonaises, scherzos, waltzes, impromptus, nocturnes, preludes and sonatas, and they all reveal how the piano had become the perfect salon instrument.

One of Schumann's last articles as a music critic launched Johannes Brahms's career:

> Sitting at the piano, he began to reveal wonderful landscapes. We were drawn into more and more magical circles. The impression was heightened by his masterly playing, which transformed the piano into an orchestra of mourning or rejoicing voices.

Brahms was first introduced to Schumann by the young violinist Joachim. Brahms was just twenty, and had come to show Robert his compositions and seek his advice. Brahms played his music to Robert, who called Clara into the room to listen. They were both immediately struck by his genius.

Brahms could be described as a classical-romantic in that he used traditional forms with Romantic expression. His works for piano include two concertos, ballades inspired by his love

Johannes Brahms on his way to his favourite tavern, The Red Hedgehog

Frédéric Chopin, 1849

of folklore; sets of technically brilliant variations and lyrical, dreamy pieces, all of which tested not just the piano's versatility but also made great demands on the pianist.

Tchaikovsky was not an admirer of Brahms's music. He wrote in his diary of 9 October 1886:

> Played over the music of that scoundrel Brahms. What a giftless bastard! It irritates me that this self-conscious mediocrity should be recognised as genius. In comparison with him, Raff was a giant, not to mention Rubinstein, a bigger and more vital personality. Brahms is so chaotic, so dry and meaningless.

Although Tchaikovsky trained as a pianist from childhood he was never good enough to excel as a virtuoso. His family weren't interested in music and sent him to work for the minister of justice in St Petersburg. In 1863 he resigned and went to study with Anton Rubinstein. Anton's brother, Nicholay, was the finest pianist in Moscow and so, in 1874, Tchaikovsky took his First Piano Concerto to him for his comments.

Rubinstein greeted the work with total silence. Tchaikovsky stood up at the end of it and said, 'Well?' at which Rubinstein burst out with a torrent of complaints about the piece – it was commonplace, unskilfully written, and trivial. Then he realised he had gone too far. Trying to placate Tchaikovsky, he offered to play the concerto after certain changes had been made. Tchaikovsky stormed out of the room determined that he would never change a note of it – and he didn't.

It was Hans von Bülow who eventually gave it the first performance on 25 October 1875, while on tour in Boston, and conducted by a local American, Benjamin Johnson Lang. The concerto has since become one of the most popular ever written. Rubinstein later admitted he had been wrong about the work and played it several times.

During the twentieth century many new sounds and colours have been brought out of the piano. Composers like Debussy exploited its resonance by using the sustaining pedal to hold overlapping harmonies. Others have taken advantage of its rhythmic qualities as a percussive sound, and finally it has been electrified. Erik Satie was the first to mess around with the inside of the piano, putting sheets of paper between the strings for a performance of *La Piège de Meduse* in 1914. More recently, John Cage changed the sound of it by creating his 'prepared piano', attaching objects such as paper, nails, spoons, screws, bolts and even milk bottles to the strings. And the composer David Bedford asked a soprano to scream the word 'Hell' inside the piano to make the strings vibrate in his *Music for Albion Moonlight* (1956).

The ultimate in caring for a piano comes from Lamonte Young, whose *Piano Piece for David Tudor No.1* (1960) asks the pianist to: 'Bring a bale of hay and a bucket of water onto the stage for the piano to eat and drink. The performer may then feed the piano or leave it to eat by itself.'

*'Brahms had played Schumann's Piano Concerto in A minor and missed a good many notes. So in the morning of the day of the concert he went to the concert hall to practise. When I arrived at the hall I found him quite alone, working away for all he was worth on Schumann's concerto . . . he was quite red in the face . . . Seeing me beside him he said, "Really, this is too bad. Those people tonight expect to hear something especially good, and here I am likely to give them a hoggish mess. Those simple diatonic runs are exasperating. I keep saying to myself, But Johannes, pull yourself together, do play decently, but no use, it's really horrid."'*

Sir Geoge Henschel,
*Musings and Memories*
1918

*The Art of Great Piano Playing*
or
*I Wish I Was Here*
Dudley Moore

Years ago I had the temerity to ask
Arthur Rubinstein:
WHAT'S THE SECRET OF A GOOD
TECHNIQUE?
He said in a very pleasantly dismissive way
'Oh – you have a technique – just play!

So I guess you have – in a sense – to
ENGINEER YOUR OWN TECHNIQUE
Liszt, curiously, agreed with that, putting
more emphasis on tone
than purely technical preoccupations.

Adopt a
RELAXED POSTURE
at the keyboard arms a little outstretched,
wrists and fingers drooping slightly
towards the keys.

It is more important to
BE LIMBER
than strong – strength arrives anyway as you
PRACTISE TINY BITS OF MUSIC
slowly.

Find the most
COMFORTABLE POSITION
of the hands and fingers
for each tiny segment of music
that you have torn off –
Practise each hand separately
and slowly.

BE PATIENT
practise
WITH A SENSE OF BEAUTY
and slowly

DON'T THINK YOU CAN WATCH TV
WHILE PRACTISING
(even if it is Solti and Moore on the Orchestra!)
The mind has amazing stamina if involved
and
ENTHUSIASTIC
The great pianist Josef Hoffman said the key
to velocity is
SLOW PRACTICE
Well – I suppose I should go and
PRACTISE WHAT I PREACH!
S L O W L Y
S L O W L Y

# The Conductor

'*Exactly how you conduct, I don't know. It is partly conscious, partly not conscious but the basic issue is simple; you either have a talent to lead or you don't and nobody can teach you that. Watching a young conductor for five minutes you know if he is leading or swimming. The swimmer never makes it, the leader always leads. That's the first criterion.*'

Sir Georg Solti

Conducting, like most difficult things performed well, can look remarkably easy. But if you think it's just a matter of waving your arms in the air for half an hour, try holding them straight out in front of you and see how long you can keep them there! It's exhausting, even for five minutes. At least early orchestral works are quite short – only fifteen or twenty minutes long, but music dating from the mid-1800s onwards can be an hour or longer, like Mahler's Eighth Symphony for example, which is over an hour and a half in length – and operas can last up to three hours, or longer.

The conductor is therefore first an athlete. But he is much more as well. In the course of any performance he has to do the following simultaneously:

- read the music
- see over 100 musicians at once
- remember where the musicians are sitting
- keep everyone together
- beat time and control the speed
- remember what's coming next
- cue all the solo parts
- listen to the sound produced
- adjust the sound produced
- look down at the score and up at the musicians without getting lost
- make hand signals and facial expressions to the musicians to indicate the interpretation required

The craft of conducting has developed over thousands of years, growing out of various different methods of beating time and 'leading' a group of instrumentalists or singers. The figure of orchestral baton conductor we recognise today has

The word conductor comes from the Latin, *conducere*, meaning 'to lead' and in music is defined as 'A person who, principally by means of the hands or gestures of the hands and arms, leads the performance of a musical ensemble.'

really only been around for less than 200 years, originating from a time when the orchestra got larger and music became more complicated, creating a need for one person, who was not preoccupied with playing an instrument, to beat time and interpret the music.

Some of the earliest evidence that music was conducted can be seen on a Greek tablet dated 709 BC, which reads, 'The Giver of Time beats with his stave up and down in equal movements so that all might keep together.' Marcus Fabius Quintilianus wrote in 95 BC, 'Musical leaders indicate intervals (of time) by stamping their feet, also (tapping) the toes.' Choral conducting in the fifteenth and sixteenth centuries involved waving a rolled-up sheet of music in the air, or tapping a stick on the ground.

During the Baroque period, the 'musical director' was the composer employed to write music for the church, chapel, theatre or court. They would usually conduct their own music, seated at a keyboard.

C.P.E. Bach wrote in 1753, 'The tone of the keyboard correctly placed at the centre of the instrumental ensemble can be heard by all. Performers located in front of or beside the keyboard will find the simultaneous motion of both hands an inescapable visual portrayal of the beat.'

In France, it was fashionable for the lead violinist to 'conduct', using the movement of the bow to indicate the beat to the rest of the instrumental group. This was a sensible arrangement as the group consisted primarily of stringed instruments and the lead violinist could demonstrate technique and interpretation on the violin and they would all understand.

By 1790 the piano was regularly in use so Haydn conducted his London Symphonies seated at one and shared the responsibility for direction with Salomon, who also 'led' from the first violin. Mozart also conducted some of his operas seated at a keyboard. Johann Stamitz in Mannheim, on the other hand, led from the violin, and is reported to have controlled his orchestra with 'no more than a nod of his head and the movement of his elbows.'

There were several things that contributed to the need for a conductor in addition to the main instrumental group. From the time of Mozart onwards, music took on a more complex construction, requiring careful interpretation of dynamic markings, with each instrumental section having more solo music to play. This necessitated guidance from someone standing independently of the orchestra to achieve and keep the correct balance. As the size of the orchestra increased it became unrealistic to try to play an instrument and control up to seventy people at the same time.

Carl Maria von Weber is often credited as being one of the first to conduct with a baton in the modern sense. This was in 1817. Three years later, Louis Spohr, the German violinist-conductor came to London to play with the Philharmonic Orchestra. The regular pianist-conductor offered Spohr his place at the keyboard, but Spohr declined, and instead stood in front of the orchestra as conductors do now.

The arrival of the conductor with a baton aroused some antagonism at first from the orchestral players, who preferred to be led by the first violin or keyboard. They complained that it was confusing and unattractive for the audience to have someone standing with his back to them, waving his arms around. Others approved of this method because at least it was silent, unlike the stick-wielding variety of conductor, who accompanied the music with thumping on the floor.

The early French conductors kept a violin handy while

The flamboyant conductor, Jullien

standing out in front of the orchestra. They probably only used it, however, to demonstrate technical points. And they used their bow not to play, but to beat time.

Eventually batons appeared, which were often heavy sticks filled with horse hair. Later, some were elaborate, highly decorated sticks, much larger and heavier than the unobtrusive modern baton. The conductor emerged as a romantic virtuoso figure, and the Italian term Maestro was coined to describe a conductor of great excellence. In Italy the Maestro had originally been the person to play the keyboard. Eventually, the Maestro took over the role of baton conducting, probably as a result of the influence of Italian opera, where it was easier and more convenient for the composer-pianist to direct the singers and orchestra, the piano providing a more central position than the violin.

Some of the early, well-known conductors took full advantage of their position in front of the orchestra to give staggering virtuoso performances. The Frenchman, Jullien, a great entertainer, is said to have worn a pair of white gloves and used a large bejewelled baton. Very good-looking and well dressed, women adored him and he knew it. Jullien's greatest success was in England between 1840 and 1859. The newspapers reported that people attended the concerts more to watch him conduct than to listen to the music, mesmerised by his long romantic curls and dark eyes. He, in turn, took advantage of this attention, using a golden music stand, dressing stylishly and presenting portraits of himself to the ladies in the dress circle. Not only eccentric, he was reportedly a good conductor, but went mad and died in a mental asylum aged forty-eight.

From 1800 onwards, conducting came to be regarded as an important profession in its own right. Both composers and performers took up the baton and took their new role as seriously as they did their writing or playing. Spontini, Spohr, Mendelssohn, Weber, Hans von Bülow, Liszt, Wagner, Mahler, Strauss, Berlioz, Furtwängler, Toscanini, are just some of the familiar names who established and developed the conductor's role.

Composers even wrote books on conducting. Berlioz included instructions on the art in his *Treatise on Orchestration*; Richard Wagner expressed his own firm ideas; and, in about 1922, Richard Strauss produced *Ten Golden Rules for Young Conductors*:

1 Remember that you are making music not to amuse yourself but to delight your audience.

Caricature of Berlioz conducting one of his 'monster' concerts

2 You should not perspire when conducting; only the audience should get warm.

3 Conduct *Salomé* and *Elektra* as if they were Mendelssohn's Fairy Music.

4 Never look encouragingly at the brass, except with a short glance to give them an important cue.

5 But never let the horns and woodwind out of your sight: if you can hear them at all, they are too strong.

6 If you think the brass is blowing hard enough, tone it down a shade or two.

7 It is not enough that you yourself should hear every word the soloist sings – you know it off by heart anyway: the

audience must be able to follow without effort. If they do not understand the words, they will go to sleep.

8 Always accompany a singer in such a way that he can sing without effort.

9 When you think you have reached the limits of prestissimo, double the pace.

10 If you follow these rules carefully you will, with your fine gifts and your great accomplishments, always be the darling of your listeners.

Strauss's first tone poem, *Don Juan*, was completed in 1889 when he was twenty-five years old.

Don Juan was a legendary figure in folklore, but Strauss based his work on a poem by the Austrian Nikolaus Lenau, the unfinished version of which was published in 1854 three years after the poet's death. The work is in one movement lasting about fifteen minutes. It opens with Don Juan pursuing numerous women. The leaping tunes represent feelings of masculine strength and vigour, the desire for new conquests. There are then tender love scenes, but increasingly, some of the victims of his actions catch up with him and so, too, does his conscience. Don Juan finds himself haunted by the ghosts of the women he has rejected and despairs that his passion has led to the pain of others. He goes to a carnival, where he is challenged to a duel by Don Pedro, someone he has wronged in the past. Realising that only death offers a way out – a fate he accepts willingly – he throws himself on Don Pedro's sword, dying to the final sinister notes of the piece.

Two months after the first performance, Hans von Bülow, Strauss's teacher, conducted *Don Juan*, but the composer was

Despite being acclaimed now, Strauss was not always popular with his contemporaries. Cesar Cui judged, 'His absurd cacophony will not be music in the thirtieth century,' and Stravinsky described the opera *Der Rosenkavalier* as 'cheap and poor'.

The following extracts appear at the front of the score for *Don Juan*:

Fain would I run the magic circle, immeasurably wide, of beautiful women's manifold charms, in full tempest of enjoyment, to die of a kiss at the mouth of the last one. O my friend, would that I could fly through every place where beauty blossoms, fall on my knees before each one, and, were it but for a moment, conquer . . .

I shun satiety and the exhaustion of pleasure; I keep myself fresh in the service of beauty; and in offending the individual I rave for my devotion to her kind. The breath of a woman that is as the odour of spring today, may perhaps tomorrow oppress me like the air of a dungeon. When, in my changes, I travel with my love in the wide circle of beautiful women, my love is a different thing for each one; I build no temple out of ruins. Indeed, passion is always and only the new passion; it cannot be carried from this one to that; it must die here and spring anew there; and, when it knows itself, then it knows nothing of repentance. As each beauty stands alone in the world, so stands the love which it prefers. Forth and away, then, to triumphs ever new, so long as youth's fiery pulses race.

It was a beautiful storm that urges me on; it has spent its rage, and silence now remains. A trance is upon every wish, every hope. Perhaps a thunderbolt from the heights which I condemned, struck fatally at my power of love and suddenly my world became a desert and darkened. And perhaps not; the fuel is all consumed and the hearth is cold and dark.

'The left hand has nothing to do with conducting. Its proper place is in the waistcoat pocket from which it should only emerge to restrain or to make some minor gesture for which in any case a scarcely perceptible glance would suffice. It is better to conduct with the ear than with the arm. The rest follows automatically.'

Richard Strauss

not impressed: 'Von Bülow has a total misconception of my work, in tempo, in everything, no inkling of poetic content . . . He introduced the public to a very interesting piece of music, but it was not *Don Juan*.' Strauss knew exactly how he wanted the piece to sound, and on another occasion shouted at the string players before the rising phrase at the beginning: 'I would ask those of you who are married to play this phrase as if you were engaged and then all will be well.'

But how does a conductor today prepare a score like *Don Juan* for performance?

The composer indicates his intentions for the piece in the front of the score, giving a list of the instruments required and, in the case of *Don Juan*, setting the scene by producing an extract from the poem on which it is based.

Further information, supplied by the publisher, includes details about the composer himself, the opus number of the work (composer's works are usually given a number indicating the order in which they were written, as far as is known) and the relevance of certain musical markings. It is important for the conductor to determine the difference between the composer's intentions and those instructions put in later by the publisher. Often, the conductor will carry out research to establish the composer's true intentions, looking at the original score if available.

It is fashionable nowadays to perform music with an authentic orchestra, meaning that the conductor uses the number and the type of instruments the composer would have originally intended.

The number of strings is determined by the conductor's interpretation of the correct requirements for the piece, often standardised as follows:

Conducting styles, like everything else, are affected by fashion. Conducting without a score became fashionable perhaps because of Toscanini, whose eyesight was so bad he couldn't read the music on the podium so he managed without it. This gave the false impression that to be a great conductor you have to work without the score!

*Right* Toscanini in a series of typical poses

*Below* Leonard Bernstein

| Classical work | Late – Romantic or modern work |
|---|---|
| 14 first violins | 18 first violins |
| 12 second violins | 16 second violins |
| 10 violas | 14 violas |
| 8 cellos | 12 cellos |
| 6 double basses | 10 double basses |

*Right* Extract from Sir Georg Solti's copy of the score of *Don Juan*

The other players in a standard modern symphony orchestra are: 2 flutes, 2 oboes, 2 clarinets, 2 bassoons, 4 horns, 4 trumpets, 3 trombones, tuba, timpani and percussion. To this might be added 2 harps, piano, cor anglais, piccolo, or two more players in each of the woodwind and brass sections.

In *Don Juan*, Strauss writes for strings, 3 flutes and a piccolo, 2 oboes and cor anglais, 2 clarinets, 2 bassoons, contra-bassoon, 4 horns, 2 trumpets, 3 trombones, tuba, harp and a percussion section of 3 timpani, glockenspiel, triangle and cymbals. It is usual to double the woodwind, brass and have 2 harps in modern performance.

There is now a standard method for laying out musical parts in an orchestral score. The woodwind are at the top, the brass second, percussion in the middle and strings at the bottom. This standard format enables the conductor to find the instruments in the score at a glance.

Before the conductor rehearses with the orchestra, he must analyse and memorise the score, going through it carefully in order to understand instructions about dynamics, interpretation and so on.

Sir Georg Solti says: 'I used to learn scores at the piano but then I found it was like taking morphine. You play and you think it's wonderful, but you realise you don't hear it in your head . . . You must go through the slow procedure of sitting

Throughout a score there are markings, often in Italian, to indicate how the music should sound. For instance:

| | | |
|---|---|---|
| ff | fortissimo | extremely loud |
| f | forte | loud |
| mf | mezzo forte | moderately loud |
| p | piano | soft |
| pp | pianissimo | very softly |
| mp | mezzo piano | moderately softly |
| cresc | crescendo | getting louder |
| dim | diminuendo | getting softer |
| sf | sforzando | suddenly loud |
| Allegro | | lively and cheerful |
| Allegretto | | not as fast as allegro |
| Agitato | | agitated |
| Andante | | gently |
| Cantabile | | singing tone |
| Amoroso | | tenderly |
| Giocoso | | humorous |
| Grazioso | | elegant |
| Largo | | slow and stately |
| Legato | | smoothly |
| Lento | | slow |
| Maestoso | | majestic |
| Marcato | | emphasised |
| Rallentando | | gradually slowing down |
| Ritenuto | | held back |
| Sostenuto | | sustained |
| Vivace | | lively |

# DON JUAN

Richard Strauss, Op.20

11090

Copyright 1904 by Jos. Aibl Verlag, Leipzig.
Renewal 1932 by C.F. Peters, Leipzig.

## Great Conductors Of The Past

| | | | |
|---|---|---|---|
| Gustav Mahler | 1860–1911 | Ernest Ansermet | 1883–1969 |
| Richard Strauss | 1864–1949 | Wilhelm Furtwängler | 1886–1954 |
| Arthur Nikisch | 1855–1922 | Arturo Toscanini | 1887–1957 |
| Felix Weingartner | 1863–1942 | Fritz Reiner | 1888–1963 |
| Sir Henry Wood | 1869–1944 | Sir Adrian Boult | 1889–1983 |
| Willem Mengelberg | 1871–1951 | Erich Kleiber | 1890–1956 |
| Serge Koussevitsky | 1874–1951 | Georg Szell | 1897–1970 |
| Pierre Monteux | 1875–1964 | Sir John Barbirolli | 1899–1970 |
| Bruno Walter | 1876–1962 | Antal Dorati | 1906–1989 |
| Sir Thomas Beecham | 1879–1961 | Herbert von Karajan | 1908–1989 |
| Leopold Stokowski | 1882–1977 | Leonard Bernstein | 1918–1990 |
| Otto Klemperer | 1885–1973 | | |

*Above* Five of the world's greatest conductors, left to right, Bruno Walter, Arturo Toscanini, Erich Kleiber, Otto Klemperer, Wilhelm Furtwängler at a desk and reading the score . . .First I read the score note by note, bar by bar. Nothing more than that. Not even forming some kind of mental image of it. Just reading. I have to be very methodical because if I know I have 200 pages to learn I will never even start! But if I know I must learn twenty pages a day for ten days, then I can do it. After twenty pages I have to get up and move around, because it's high, difficult concentration. I don't have a photographic memory and envy people who do because it helps you learn more quickly.

'Then I read it again, maybe four or five times. After this I begin to imagine the form of the piece, how it should sound. I read it again and this time I start singing, conducting, making noises, imagining the speed, dynamics. When I feel I know it, only then do I listen to a recording.

'I have two professions – conducting concerts and opera and, more recently, playing the piano again. Between them there is a very large repertoire of music. After ten years, say, when I see a score again, I have to re-learn it, as if I had never seen it before. As I have no photographic memory, I am usually left with a kind of faded xerox copy in my head. I have to start again, learning it intensively. This is partly a disadvantage, but mostly an advantage, because it means I have to learn the music again from scratch and ten years on, I can bring some new experience to it.'

No performance can go ahead without rehearsal. As rehearsing is an expensive business, it is not unusual for the conductor and orchestra to have very few rehearsals together before a concert. Meeting the orchestra for the first time is an important moment – the musicians may be wary – Do they know the conductor by reputation? What is he like? Is he good?

As Sir Georg Solti says: 'Orchestras will not collaborate

with you because you are rich or poor or good-looking. An orchestra likes you only if you are a good conductor and a good musician and you prove it. If they don't like you, if they hate you, you don't get any result. That's a hard thing.'

Communication between the players and conductor is all-important. They must be able to see and feel in touch with each other if they are to perform well together. The layout of the orchestra must be consistent so the conductor knows without hesitation where a particular player is sitting.

Sir Georg gives Dudley some advice on how to conduct *Don Juan* for the first time:

1 The first ingredient you need to be a conductor is to be a maniac about it. You must really believe in what you are doing. You cannot conduct if you have inhibitions.

2 You must have an ability to plunge yourself into the music, especially with a score like *Don Juan*, which is extremely passionate.

3 Before you start, close your eyes and imagine the tempo in your mind. Keep still, don't move your hands or arms, or you will confuse the musicians.

4 A good upbeat is all it takes, but you must always keep the tempo in mind. When you are beating in two, the one is a luxury, the two is the business.

5 You can beat with your fingers, wrist, your eyes, foot, it really doesn't matter, as long as you have imagination and know what you want.

6 Don't expect miracles. There are no short cuts. I have fought for forty-five years to get the down beat and up beat right at the beginning of *Don Juan*.

*'As soon as Solti walks through the door, there is an electric atmosphere all over the theatre. The place gets charged. And I can't help feeling that if it were possible to plug him into the general circuit, you could turn off the mains and light the whole house with his own electricity.'*

A technician at the
Royal Opera House,
London

7 The metronome is one of the conductor's closest friends. The speed must be right. Too slow it will sound stodgy, too fast and some of the parts will be unplayable.

8 Control the tempo. Holding the speed is very important. You must have a clock inside you – in your body.

9 You must know the music inside out otherwise your head will be buried in the score and that's no good.

10 If you are working with an orchestra you don't know, the first thing you must do is look around and ask who is playing first, where are they sitting. You must know where everyone is sitting.

11 Remember that we are working in a large studio and the orchestra is very spread out. By the time the sound reaches you from the back it is already late. You must get them to play on the beat so they don't drag behind.

12 Know when to watch and when to listen. Be 'in' and 'out' of the music.

13 When things aren't working out you must know how to diagnose what is wrong. And say how to correct it. One small thing going wrong can throw the whole orchestra. You must try to understand how the musician's mind works and how each instrument will respond to the person who's trying to make certain technical demands on it.

14 The orchestra/conductor relationship is like the lion and the tamer. As long as the tamer is firm, the lion doesn't eat him up. I prefer to be thought of as a respected friend.

15 Preparation is everything. If you have prepared everything and rehearsed properly, you should be able to enjoy the concert because the work is done.

'I was twelve years old in Budapest and I went to a concert. Erich Kleiber was conducting – a great talent, a marvellous conductor. It was a Beethoven concert and they played Beethoven's Fifth Symphony. I sat there in a magical trance – I went out at the end and said, "This is my life." I went home to my mother, who was my musical mentor, and said, "Mother, I want to be a conductor," and she made the absolutely classic, philosophical remark of a Jewish mother: "OK, that's fine, but first go and do your piano practice."'

Sir Georg Solti

'I've never wanted to be a conductor because I don't feel it is in my make-up, whereas with you [Solti], I feel it is an extension of you. Maybe it's just that I heard too much music on the radio and never had your early experience of seeing conductors live.'

Dudley Moore

But there's one final word:

I don't find conducting technically difficult now because I have learnt it over the years, but the most difficult thing is that you must never be totally satisfied with a performance. You must always develop, try harder when you do a piece again. I dread the day I can say, 'It was very good yesterday,' because I know that would be the end.

---

# *Appendix*

## Recommended Listening

The pieces below all come from the television series and are simply an introduction to the composers' works.

### The Baroque

Johann Sebastian Bach, *The Brandenburg Concertos/ Concerto in D minor for two violins*
George Frideric Handel, *Grand Concertos op.6, No. 11*

### The Classical Era

Joseph Haydn, *Symphony No. 99 ('London')*
Wolfgang Amadeus Mozart, *Overture to The Marriage of Figaro*
Ludwig van Beethoven, *Symphony No. 9 ('Choral')*
Franz Schubert, *Symphony No. 8. ('Unfinished')*

### The Romantics

Hector Berlioz, *Symphonie fantastique*
Robert Schumann, *Piano Concerto in A minor*
Johannes Brahms, *St Antony Variations (two versions – for orchestra and for two pianos)*
Richard Wagner, *Prelude to Die Meistersinger*
Richard Strauss, *Don Juan*
Peter Ilyich Tchaikovsky, *Piano Concerto No. 1*

### The Twentieth Century

Igor Stravinsky, *The Rite of Spring*
Maurice Ravel, *La Valse*
Béla Bartók, *Music for Strings, Percussion and Celeste*
Witold Lutoslawski, *Symphony No. 3*

## Bibliography/Recommended Reading

*Guinness Book of Music*, Robert and Celia Deavling (Guinness Books)
*Orchestral Performance Practice*, Daniel Koury (U.M.I. Research Press)
*Orchestration: Beethoven to Berlioz*, Adam Carse (C.U.P.)
*Orchestration of the Eighteenth Century*, Adam Carse (C.U.P.)
*Musical Bumps*, Dudley Moore (Robson)
*An Illustrated History of Musical Instruments*, Mary Remnant (Batsford)
*The New Music, the Avant-Garde since 1945*, Reginald Smith Brindle (Oxford University Press)
*Beecham Stories*, ed. Atkins and Newman (Robson)
*Words About Music*, John Amis and Michael Rose (Faber)
*Hector Berlioz, Memoirs*, trans. David Cairns (Panther)
*Stravinsky, Memories and Commentaries*, ed. Robert Craft (Faber)
*The Musician's World: Letters of the Great Composers*, ed. Hans Gal (Thames & Hudson)
*The Book of Musical Anecdotes*, Norman Lebrecht (Sphere)
*Letters of Wolfgang Amadeus Mozart*, ed. Hans Mersman (Dover)
*Joseph Haydn, Collected Correspondence*, ed. H. C. Robbins Landon (Barrie & Rockliff)
*Classical Music Lists*, Herbert Kupferberg (Ward Lock)
*Conversations with Witold Lutoslawski*, Bàlint Andràs Varga (Chester)
*Good Music Guide*, Neville Garden (Bloomsbury)
*Bach*, Denis Arnold (Oxford University Press)
*Life of Ludwig van Beethoven*, trans. Henry E. Krehbiel (Centaur Press)

*Mozart in Vienna*, Volkmar Braunbehrens (André Deutsch)

*Handel*, Christopher Hogwood (Thames & Hudson)

*Haydn, His Life and Music*, H. C. Robbins Landon (Thames & Hudson)

*Gustav Mahler; Memories and Letters*, trans. Basil Creichton, ed. Donald Mitchell (John Murray)

*Mozart, The Golden Years*, H. C. Robbins Landon (Thames & Hudson)

*1791, Mozart's Last Year*, H. C. Robbins Landon (Thames & Hudson)

*Galina, A Russian Story* (the personal story of the singer, Galina Vishnevskaya, wife of Mstislav Rostropovich) (Sceptre)

*Broadwood By Appointment*, David Wainwright (Quiller Press)

*A Study of Orchestra*, Samuel Adler (musical examples from text available on CD) (Norton)

*A Dictionary of Musical Quotations*, Ian Crofton and Donald Fraser (Routledge)

*A History of Western Music*, Donald J. Grout (Dent)

*Kobbe's Complete Opera Book*, ed. The Earl of Harwood (Bodley Head)

*Instruments of the Orchestra*, John Hosier (Oxford University Press)

*The New Harvard Dictionary of Music*, ed. Don Randel (Belknap Harvard)

*The Cambridge Music Guide*, ed. Stanley Sadie (Cambridge University Press)

*The New Grove Dictionary of Music*, ed. Stanley Sadie (20 vols, but there is also the condensed version, *The Grove Concise Dictionary of Music*) (Macmillan)

## Museums and Galleries   Where to see musical instruments:

The Ulster Museum
Botanic Gardens
Belfast BT9 5AB
Tel: 0232 381251

Bolling Hall Museum
Bolling Hall Road
Bradford BD4 7LP
Tel: 0274 723057

Fitzwilliam Museum
Trumpington Street
Cambridge CB2 1RB
Tel: 0223 332900
(strings and keyboards)

National Museum of Wales
Cathays Park
Cardiff CF1 3NP
Tel: 0222 569441

Edinburgh University
Reid Concert Hall
Bristol Square
Edinburgh EH8 9AG
Tel: 031-667 1011

Royal Museum of Scotland
Chambers Street
Edinburgh EH1 1JF
Tel: 031-225 7534

Glasgow Art Gallery & Museum
Kelvingrove
Glasgow G3 8AG
Tel: 041-357 3929

Tolson Museum
Ravensknowle Park
Wakefield Road
Huddersfield HD5 8DJ
Tel: 0484 530591

Liverpool Museum
William Brown Street
Liverpool L3 8EN
Tel: 051-207 0001

Fenton House
Hampstead Grove
London NW3
Tel: 081-435 3471
(early keyboard instruments)

Horniman Museum & Library
London Road
London SE23
Tel: 081-699 1872
(large collection of instruments from all over the world)

The Musical Museum
368 High Street
Brentford
Middx TW8 0EF
Tel: 081-560 8108
(keyboard instruments)

Victoria & Albert Museum
Cromwell Road
London SW7
Tel: 071-938 8500
(comprehensive collection)

The Ashmolean Museum
Beaumont Street
Oxford OX1 2PH
Tel: 0865 278000
(stringed instruments & bows)

University Faculty of Music
The Bate Collection
St Aldate's
Oxford OX1 1DB
Tel: 0865 270927

Organ Museum
320 Camp Road
St Albans AL1 5PB
Tel: 0727 51557

Castle Museum
York YO1 1RY
Tel: 0904 653611

# A selection of composers' homes and museums

*America*
Smithsonian Museum, Washington DC (instruments)
The Shrine to Music Museum, Vermillion, Dakota
The Metropolitan Museum, New York (instruments)
Percy Grainger's House, New York (also in Sydney, Australia)
Morgan Library, New York
Museum of the American Piano, New York
UCLA Collection, Los Angeles

*Austria*
Richard Strauss' house, House Garmisch, Bavarian Alps
Mozarteum, Salzburg

*England*
Elgar Birthplace Museum, Broadheath
Benjamin Britten, The Aldeburgh Foundation, The Maltings, Snape, Suffolk
Beecham Archive, Denton, Norfolk
Handel Collection, The British Library, London

*Finland*
Sibelius' house, Turku

*France*
Bibliothèque Nationale, Department de la Musique, Paris

Bibliothèque Nationale du Conservatoire, Paris
Bibliothèque Municipale, Palace of Versailles
Ravel's home, The Belvedere, Monfort l'Amaury, nr Paris

*Germany*
Handel's house, Halle
Beethoven's house, Bonn
Wagner's house, Wahnfried, The Wagner Museum, Bayreuth
Bach Archiv, Leipzig
Thomasschule (Bach), Leipzig
The German Museum, Nuremberg

*Hungary*
Liszt Academy, Budapest
National Museum of Hungary, Budapest (Liszt & Beethoven)
Esterhàza Palace

*Italy*
Monteverdi's grave, Church Santa Maria Gloriosa Dei Frari, Venice
Casa Goldoni, Venice
Museum of Stradivarius, Cremona
Conservatoire di Musica Luigi Cherubini, Florence (instruments)
Verdi's house, Sant'Agata, nr Palma

*Switzerland*
Stravinsky Archive, Basle

# Author's Acknowledgements

This book has involved a special commitment from many people, for which I am most grateful. My own personal inspiration came from Jonathan Hewes and Susanna Yager, who always showed total faith in me. It also came from hearing the composers' music played by Dud, Sir Georg and the Band, who entertained us all during the filming of the series with the most exceptional music-making.

I would like to thank the many people who have given me their support, advice and encouragement: Susanna Yager, Jonathan Hewes and Rupert Lancaster, for giving this important opportunity to a new author; Zafer Baran, David Farrell, Amanda Horton, Dudley Moore, Charles Kaye, Kate Poole and Sir Georg Solti, for their help in creating the book. Thanks also to Jonathan Burton, Nobby Clark, John Goodwin, Martyn Hayes Associates, Bill Hogan, Han Huang, Nicholas John, Geoffrey and Helen Keating, Declan Lowney, Avril MacRory, Professor Rosamond McGuinness, Peter McInerney (S. J. Berwins), Sylvia Morris, Rachel Portman, the staff of the Schleswig Holstein Orchestra, Phillippa Thomson, Elaine Walmsley and the Younghusband and Dibnah families, especially my parents, who have always encouraged me to love music. I am especially grateful to Sue Sutherley for her support and advice in organising the musical information.

Many thanks to the following institutions for their help and cooperation with research materials: John D. Broadwood and Sons, The British Library, The British Museum Information Centre, The American Music Centre (New York), the City of Westminster and Barbican Libraries, and Steinway and Sons (London).

The Schleswig Holstein Music Festival Orchestra
*Violins* Jonas Alber, Ralph Allen, Annedore Hein, Dorisz Batka, Roswitha Devrient, Benedikt Fischer-Bruedern, Dionisia Fernandez, Uta Heidemann, Laura Hilgeman, Susan Hytken, Maarten Jansen, Inna Kogan, Dorit Koepping, Taras Krysa, Peter Krysa, Laurie Landers, Barbara Littman, Kotowa Machida, Volker Moeller, Witali Nedin, Marina Reshetowa, Regina Sarkissowa, Melinda Scott, Anne-Katrin Seidel, Olaf Spies, Susanne Scholz, Armin Schubert, Brigitte Stoeppler, Linda Wang, Grace Wang, Marina Waletowa, Bing Wang, Lin Wang, Johannes Watzel, Bagus Wiswakarma.

*Violas* Viktor Chen, Dirk Hegemann, Sebastian Herberg, Chen-Hung Ho, Arthur Holdys, Jone Kaliunaite, Antje Kaufmann, Richard Kessler, Ilze Klishane, John Largess, Mercedes Leon, Alisa Meves, Anne-Marie Miller, Lothar Weiche.

*Cellos* Alexander Bagrinzew, Reinis Birznieks, Pansy Chang, Sanne DeGraaf, Lars Kristiansson, Andrea Laszlo, Susan Lerner, Ringela Riemke, Joanna Sachryn, Alexander Snatschjenok, Tim Stolzenburg, Sofia Zappi.

*Double Basses* Ekkehard Beringer, Ruediger Dierks, Todd Doty, Anthony Leon Manzo, Claus Peter Nebelung, Cornelia Roth, Michael Sandronow, Axel Scherka, Waldemar Schweirtz, Andrej Teplov, Raymond Vargas.

*Flutes* Ulrike Gaetzner, Constanze Knoefel, Ingo Nelken, Iris Wimmer, Dorothee Wulle.

*Oboes* Helen Devilleneuve, Olivier Doise, Markus Goetzinger, Christoph Hartmann, Thomas Hipper.

*Clarinets* Peter Landers, Andreas Lehnert, Staffan Martensson, Bernhard Nusser, Albert Osterhammer.

*Bassoons* Lucius Hemmer, Annet Karsten, David Petersen, Bernhard Straub, Jiping Tan.

*Horns* Eric Borninkhof, Suzanne George, Thomas Hauschild, Guido Hendriks, René Pagen, Claudia Strenkert, Viesturs Vardaunis, Christian Wagner.

*Trumpets* Britta Corell, Martin Friess, Hub Nickel, Cyrille van Poucke, Volker Siepelt.

*Trombones* Stefan Geiger, Heinrich Goelzenleuchter, Martin Hofmeyer, Bjoern Koschmieder.

*Tubas* Edwin Diefes, Herbert Waldner.

*Percussion* Thomas Hoefs, Herbert von Reibnitz, Stefan Rapp, Thomas Siahaan, Adam Weisman, Dirk Wucherpfennig.

*Pianists* Ellen Braslavsky, Emiko Hori.

*Harps* Heike Bergmann, Valeria Madini-Moretti.

*The Administration of the Schleswig Holstein Festival* Ruediger Schramm (Managing Director), Frank Horx, Cathrin Rehder, Evelyne Ferry, Helen Kindermann, Inga Hildebrand, Marjorie Elickson, Kerstin Ulrich, Karin Frieling, Silke Dittmann, Thomas Hanelt, Stefan Fink, Olaf Grulke, Axel Petrick, Joachim Krause, Henrik Schueler. *Conductors* Stefan Malzew, Gilbert Varga.

*Sir Georg Solti's Office* Charles Kaye (Secretariat) and Deborah Jones

*For the series 'ORCHESTRA!'*, Initial Film and Television Executive Producer, Malcolm Gerrie; Producer, Jonathan Hewes; Director, Declan Lowney; Director of Photography and Lighting Designer, Nic Knowland; Lighting Designer, Patrick Marks; Design, Michael Minas; Editor, Tim Wadell; Sound Director, Roy Drysdale; Production Manager, Jenny King.

*UK production team* Mike Amos, Jeff Baynes, Susie Boyle, Eddie Bramfitt, James Brown, Susannah Buxton, Peter Cavaciutti, Dave Chapman, Lee Cleary, Monica Cowley, Pamela Cummins, Andy Curling, Roger Dawson, John Dunkerley, Bob Eames, David Farrell, Bob Freeman, Clive Freeth, Marcia Gay, Erik Gibbons, Donal Gilligan, Peter Harris, Chris Hazell, Miec Heggett, Ian Howard, Han Huang, Gerard Johnson, Jenny King, Brogan Lane, Colm Lowney, Avril MacRory, Kay Mander, Mira Minas, Andy Moore, Jane Moorfoot, Brian Morris, Trevor Murphy, Eugene O'Connor, Nick Palmer, Chris Plevin, Elmer Postle, Robert Pye, Luke Rainey, Kelvin Richard, Mike Rickard, Adam Rickets, Andy Rose, Julie Sheppard, Simon Smith, Peter Soole, Bobby Stagg, Adam Stevenson, Tim Wadell, Elaine Walmsley, Grace Wells, John Whitby, Jeff Woolbridge, Susan Young, Michael Zimbrich.

*German Production team* Andrea Domizlaff, Peter Fink, Tanya Franke, Petra Gaffke, Beatrice Hanke, Manfred Hanke, Susanne Kaiser, Tommy Kroepels, Manfred Lenert, Brigitta Luettge, Nabil Ali Moghib, Karl Petrie, Ole Reuss, Anna-Carina Schonn, Uli Schroder, Stephanie Stocker, Corinna Triimborn, Gunnar Windelband, Thomas Zastko.

# Photographic Acknowledgements

The author and publisher would like to thank the following for supplying and granting permission to reproduce illustrations, listed by page number, with special thanks to Leon Meyer of The Hulton Picture Company and Paul Collen of The Royal College of Music.

Archiv Für Kunst und Geschichte Berlin 109; Biblioteca Apostolica Vaticana 17; Chicago Symphony Orchestra 155; The Hulton Picture Company 13a, 14, 15, 16, 27ab, 33, 34, 49, 52, 61ab, 65, 69, 70, 84, 87, 89b, 95b, 102, 109bc, 126, 127, 140, 141ab, 142, 143, 145, 171b, 177a, 183a, 193, 199, 202; Hulton Picture Company/Bettmann Archive 99, 129, 146, 148; Mansell Collection 7, 22, 25, 46, 48, 75, 89a, 94, 104, 132, 135, 183b, 197; Mary Evans Picture Library 6, 13b, 20ab, 39, 50, 62, 66, 68, 95a, 136, 174, 177, 184, 195, 199; Peters Edition Ltd., 149, 150b, 154; Roger Viollet Paris 171b; Royal College of Music 24, 54, 91, 100, 107, 131, 138, 139, 150a, 185.

Line illustrations: Zafer Baran

# Index

Page numbers in italics indicate captions

atonality 148

Bach, C. P. E. 39, 40, 172, 191
Bach, J. C. 49, 170
Bach, Johann Sebastian 18, 20–3, *20*, 21, *21*, 91, 117, 129, 168–9
ballet 14, 124–8, 131, 145
Baroque period 4, 7, 9–35, 121
Bartók, Béla 135–8, 138, 143
bassoon 15, 16, 40, 56, 72, 78–9
Bedford, David 186
Beethoven, Ludwig van 34, 35, 38, 58–68, 82, 86, 87, 96, 101, 148, 172, 174–6
   scores 129, *174*
Berberian, Cathy: score *151*
Berg, Alban 148
Berio, Lucio 151
Berkeley, Michael 152, 154
Berlioz, Hector 33–4, 71, 76, 78, 83, 86, 87, 88–91, *88*, 117, 118, 131, 182, 184, 194, *195*
Bernstein, Leonard *146*, 147, 150, *199*, 202
Birtwistle, Harrison 152
Boulanger, Nadia 151
Boulez, Pierre 149, 151
bow 31, 32
Brahms, Johannes 87, 94–6, 134, 182, 184–5, *184*, 186
brass instruments 81, 83, 112–19
Britten, Benjamin 122, 140, *141*
Bruckner, Anton 86, 87, 101, 103, *107*
Bülow, Hans von 96, 97, 107, 186, 194, 196–8
Buxtehude, Dietrich 19–20

Cage, John 41, 123, 147, 149–50, 155, 186
   scores *149*, *154*
Carter, Elliott 41, *144*, 146
Cavalli, Francesco 13

cello 4, 28–30, 32, 34
chamber music 16, 40, 69
Charles II 15–16
Chopin, Frederic 87, 182–4, *185*
chordaphone 30
clarinet 18, 40, 43, 56, 72, 74, 77–8, 114
clarino 117
Classical period 7, 37–79, 121
clavichord 166
Clementi, Muzio 66
concerto 17–18, 26, 41–3, 50–1, 118
concerts 38, 39–40, 82, 84–6
conductor 91–2, 97–8, 101, 147, 172, 189–208
contrabassoon 79
Copland, Aaron 128, *143*, 144–5
cor anglais 72, 77, 83
Corelli, Arcangelo 17, 26

da Ponte, Lorenzo 51
Dallapiccola, Luigi 18
Debussy, Claude 124, *129*, 133–4, 176, 186
Diaghilev, Sergei 124, 127, 131, 132, 133
divertimenti 47
Dolmetsch, Arnold 155
double bass 4, 28, 35
drums 156, 158–60
Dvořák, Anton 83, 134–5, 143

electronic music 150, 151
Elgar, Edward 138, *138*
Enlightenment 38, 48
Esterhazy family 44–6, 54, 56–8
Expressionism 148

'Five, The' 135
Florentine Camerata 11
flute 15, 40, 56, 72, 74–6
folk songs 134, 138, 144
Frederick the Great of Prussia *75*, 76
Furtwängler, Wilhelm 194, 202, *202*

Gay, John 25
George III *39*
Gershwin, George 122, 145
Giustini, Ludovico 172
Gluck, Christoph Willibald 24, *24*, 40
Grainger, Percy 147

Handel, George Frideric 20, *20*, 23–7, *24*, 58
harp 30, 83
harpsichord 12, 30, 46, 166–8, *166*, 172
Haydn, Joseph 34, 38, 44–9, *46*, *48*, 51, 53, 54, 54–8, 59, 84–6, 172
   score *43*
Hindemith, Paul 128
Hogarth, William: *The Chorus 6*
Holst, Gustav 123, 138–9, 143
Honegger, Arthur 134
horn 40, 112–14
Horowitz, Vladimir 170
Hotteterre, Jean 15, 74, 77
*House Rules and Maxims for Young Musicians* 7, 178

Ives, Charles 143–4

Joachim, Joseph 96
Jullien, Louis Antoine *193*, 194

Kleiber, Erich 202, *202* 207
Klemperer, Otto 136, 202, *202*

Lieder 41, 68–9
lira da braccio 28
Liszt, Franz 87, 92–4, 108–10, 176–7, *177*, 179, 182, 183, 184, 194
Louis XIV 13–14, 74
Lully, Jean-Baptiste 13–15, *15*, 74, 114
Luther, Martin 10, 19
Lutoslawski, Witold 154–5, *155*

Mahler, Gustav 71, 86, 87, 100, 101–3, 111, 190, 194, 202
Mendelssohn Bartholdy, Felix 87, 91–2, *91*, 110–11, 183, 194
Messaien, Oliver 150–1, *151*
Meyerbeer, Giacomo 110
Milhaud, Darius 134
minimalism 149, 152
Monteux, Pierre 127, 128, 202
Monteverdi, Claudio 12–13
Mozart, Constanze 52, 53–4
Mozart, Leopold 51, 53
Mozart, Wolfgang Amadeus 33, 39, 43, 44, 47, *48*, 49–55, *51*, 59, 71, 78, 79, 117, 129, 172–3
musical director 12, 191
musical terms 200

nationalism 134–6
Neo-Classicism 128
Nielsen, Carl 135
notation 152, *154*

oboe 15, 16, 40, 56, 72, 74, 76–8
oboe da caccia 77
oboe d'amore 18, 77
ondes martenot 145, 151
opera 11
  Baroque 12–15, 16, 24, 25
  Classical 40, 50, 51–3, 66
  Romantic 86, 98, 104–8
  20th century 98, 122, 134, 140
ophicleide 118
orchestra 4, 43, 84–6, 88, 155, 200
  layout *31*, *75*, 86, *115*
organ 19

Paganini, Nicolò 30, 33–34, *33*, 90
percussion 123, *154*, 156–63
Philidor, Michel 15, 74
piano 30, 46, 50, 83, 154, 165–87, 191–2, 193
piccolo 72, 76
Poulenc, Francis 88, 134
*Principles of Orchestration* 135
Prokofiev, Sergei 128, 142
Purcell, Henry 16, 77

Quantz, J. J. 38, 40, 76
quartets 40, 48–9, 66

Rachmaninov, Sergey 135, *135*

Raff, Joachim 185
Ravel, Maurice 130–3, *131*, 134, 145, 172
rebec 28
reeds 77, 78
Renaissance period 7, 121
Rogers, Richard 41
Romantic period 7, 34, 65, 81–119, 121, 166
Rostropovich, Mstislav *34*
Rubinstein, Nikolay 100, 185–6

sackbut 118
Saint-Saëns, Camille 35, 128
Salieri, Antonio 53, 55, 71
Salomon, Johann Peter 47, 54–5, *54*
Satie, Erik 128, 134, 186
saxophone 83
Schaeffer, Pierre 150
Schoenberg, Arnold 122, 143, 145, 147–8, *148*
Schubert, Franz 41, 68, *68*, *69*, 87, 101, 129, 183
Schumann, Clara *6*, 96, 179, 182, 183, 184
Schumann, Robert *6*, 7, 87, 91, 92, 96, 177–83, 184, 186
  score *182*
Schütz, Heinrich 19
scores: modern *151*, 152, *152*
serenade 47
serial music 148–9
serpent 25
Shostakovich, Dmitri 142, *143*
Sibelius, Jean 128, 135
sinfonia concertante 54
'Six, Les' 128, 134
Smithson, Harriet *88*, 90
Solti, Sir Georg *155*
sonata 17, 40
sonata form 42, 47
songs 40–1, 68–9
Spohr, Louis 192, 194
Stockhausen, Karlheinz 122–3, 151, 152
Strauss, Richard 83, 87, 90, 96–100, 117, 122, 139, 176, 194, 196–8, 202
  score *200*
Stravinsky, Igor 78, 122, 124–30, *129*, 131, 132, 143, 145, 196
string instruments 4, 28–35
strings: characteristics 28
symphonic poem 87, 94
symphony 41–8, 54, 60, 65–6, 69–71, 86, 92, 94, 96, 101–4, 142, 154

Tchaikovsky, Peter Ilyich 83, 100–1, *100*, 185–6
*Ten Golden Rules for Young Conductors* 194–6
theme 87–8
timpani 156, 158–60
Tippett, Sir Michael 60, 123, 140–2, *141*
tone poem 87, 98
Toscanini, Arturo 194, 199, *199*, 202, *202*
*Treatise on Orchestration* 33, 76, 90, 194
trombone 40, 71, 112, 118
trumpet 112, 114–18
tuba 112, 118–19
Twentieth century 7, 121–63

Varèse, Edgar 145–6
Vaughan Williams, Ralph 119, 123, 138, *139*
Verdi, Giuseppe 104, 108
Viennese Schools 71, 148
viol 12, 28
viola 4, 28–30, 32–4, 40, 83–4
viola da braccia 32
viola da gamba 32
viola d'amore 18
violin 4, 17, 28–32, *32*, 83–4
  conducting from 191, 192–3
violin family, *see* string instruments
'Violons du Roi' 14, *14*
violone 35
Viotti, Giovanni Battista 30
Vivaldi, Antonio *16*, 17–19, 34, 78, 79
Vogl, Johann Michael 68, *69*

Wagner, Cosima 96, 107, 108, *109*, 110
Wagner, Richard 33, 86, 87, 96, 104, 106–10, *107*, *109*, 117, 118–19, 122, 148, 176, 179, 194
Wagner tuba 110, 119
Walter, Bruno 202, *202*
Walton, Sir William 140, *140*
Weber, Carl Maria von 87–8, 192, 194
Webern, Anton 148–9, 152
Williamson, Malcolm 147
Wittgenstein, Paul 172
woodwind 14–15, 37, 47, 72–9, 83
word painting 11, 23–4

Young, Lamonte 186